Joe Bennett is an English-born author
and columnist. He has lived in Lyttelton
since 1988.

From There to Here

JOE BENNETT

HarperCollins*Publishers*

This is a work of non-fiction, but in some instances I've changed names because it's not their fault.

HarperCollins*Publishers*
Australia • Brazil • Canada • France • Germany • Holland • India
Italy • Japan • Mexico • New Zealand • Poland • Spain • Sweden
Switzerland • United Kingdom • United States of America

First published in 2023
by HarperCollinsPublishers (New Zealand) Limited
Unit D1, 63 Apollo Drive, Rosedale, Auckland 0632, New Zealand
harpercollins.co.nz

A catalogue record for this book is available from the National Library of New Zealand

ISBN 978 1 7755 4056 4 (pbk)
ISBN 978 1 7754 9093 7 (ebook)

Cover design by Louisa Maggio, HarperCollins Design Studio
Front cover image: Author's private collection
Back cover image by Daniela Aebli
Typeset in ITC Stone Serif Std by Kirby Jones
Author photograph by Daniela Aebli
Printed and bound in Australia by McPherson's Printing Group

MIX
Paper | Supporting
responsible forestry
FSC
www.fsc.org
FSC® C001695

From There to Here

Others, I am not the first,
Have willed more mischief than they durst.

A. E. Housman

Wine comes in at the mouth
And love comes in at the eye;
That's all we shall know for truth
Before we grow old and die.

W. B. Yeats

Chapter 1

My father, aged six, was bitten by a neighbour's dog. He ran home to his mother, wailing. The neighbour showed up soon after, bringing the dog along to show it was a sweet-natured beast. My grandmother hit it on the head with a rake and killed it. It's the only thing I know of my grandmother's life, and my father's youth. We are not a story-telling family.

My father was raised in Sheffield in the north of England, but if he'd ever had a Yorkshire accent he'd scrubbed it by the time I was born. We lived down south in Sussex. The north, with its cloth caps, coal mines and heavy industry, seemed as remote as Patagonia. When we once went on holiday to Scotland, my father drove through Yorkshire without stopping.

By the time I knew my grandmother her great dog-killing days were behind her. She had followed my father south and lived across the road from us, in the village of

Willingdon. To visit her was to be given a rich tea biscuit. These were kept in a round glass jar and they were soft. I got into trouble for spitting one out.

She lived in the last of a little terrace of grey cottages. Her eyes were poor and her legs dropsical. Ants and mice increasingly had the run of the place. Eventually it became clear that she could no longer keep house, and my father found her a place in an old people's home. She resisted the move, but within a week of settling in you couldn't have dragged her out. There were just so many people there to talk about. She was happy.

Until, that is, some ten years later when my father died, and she lost interest in going on. In her last months she was befriended by professional befrienders, and she left them most of what she owned. They turned up gloating to her funeral. But she did leave each of her grandchildren £200. My bequest arrived just in time to pay a fine that I couldn't otherwise have paid. I'll come to that.

I was born Julian Bennett in 1957. It was a lucky time. The post-war gloom had ended; the boom begun. I was part of an Anglo-Saxon population explosion, a subconscious urge to repopulate the country. Conditions were good for breeding, and my parents, along with a whole newly confident generation, went at it. Every house seemed to swarm with kids. I was the fourth of four. We went boy, girl, boy, boy, just like the royal family and more or less in time with them.

We lived at 2 Huggetts Lane, Willingdon. Over the road was the recreation ground. A hundred yards along Huggetts Lane, houses gave way to fields. Our house was called Ryton. I don't know why. It was large and detached, with a long back garden. The near half was lawn, the far half vegetables. Separating the two was the tallest hedge in the world. It was possible to climb up inside the hedge and emerge through the top and become emperor of everything. At the front of the house stood another wonder, the lilac tree. It could be climbed to the dizzying height of perhaps a couple of yards.

In what must have been the fabled winter of 1962–63 the snow lay deeper than I was tall, and was littered with the corpses of birds. Ice formed on the inside of the bedroom windows and we kids came down to the kitchen in the morning to dress in front of the range. This was a vast and primitive coal-fired device that seemed like the house's single vital organ, its seat of warmth and energy. That it was a temperamental beast and the bane of my mother's life never impinged on my consciousness, because nothing much did except selfish pleasures. And Mr Fisher.

Mr Fisher was the village dentist. My mother didn't drive then and my father was at work, so whenever we needed a tooth filled, which was often, we went to Mr Fisher. Though 'went' is hardly the verb. The entrance to his surgery was scored with parallel tracks carved by children approaching in the manner of dragged puppies.

He operated from his own house, with the surgery in an upstairs room, presumably to give his receptionist more chance of intercepting patients when they ran. The waiting room was the landing, and devoid of fripperies such as picture books for the children, the better for them to concentrate on the noises coming through the wall. The surgery door was an ordinary bedroom door, except for the bolt on it.

Mr Fisher must have been over sixty, which meant he would have qualified not long after the First World War. I remember him standing in front of the window in looming silhouette. Behind him, arrayed across frosted glass, ran an elaborate series of cogs and gears and chains. This dread engine was driven mechanically by a pedal under Mr Fisher's foot in order to rotate the drill in Mr Fisher's hand. I didn't wait for the drill to start to get crying. I was at it from the moment my mother unpeeled my fingers from the door jamb and lifted me into the chair for the dental assistant to pinion.

Eventually I suspect it was my mother who could take no more. She put us all on the bus to Eastbourne and took our custom to 'nice Mr Mabberley'. Mr Mabberley had a high-speed drill that ran on new-fangled electricity. And he offered anaesthetic injections in a range of flavours. I chose strawberry and could taste it. But I still cried, cried by reflex, cried in anticipation. Even today when the dentist reaches for the drill my body arcs like the Harbour Bridge.

My brother Simon was two years older, old enough to have school friends and a brick-red scooter, and I can see them now scooting away up Huggetts Lane, and me running to keep up on my fat little legs. 'Wait for me,' I wailed, 'wait for me.' Needless to say they didn't wait for me, indeed the point of their scooting was not waiting for me. They scooted around the bend towards Hampden Park and unimagined happiness, and I yearned to join them more that I thought it possible to yearn. I ached with scooter-lust. The scooter I eventually inherited, of course, was Simon's, by which time he and his friends had graduated to bikes. On which to pedal off down Huggetts Lane etc.

What I wanted was justice, and justice was defined as getting what I wanted. In this I was no more selfish than other children, but I suspect I was more persistent.

I attended a children's party, the only one I remember ever going to, around the corner in Meadows Road. It was to celebrate the birthday of a boy of about my age whom I considered fat, so he must have been effectively spherical.

There was a game supervised by Spherical's mother. I forget how it went but the rules had an obvious flaw, which I exploited to win. The prize was a sherbet fountain – a threepenny confection consisting of a cylinder of yellow cardboard full of sherbet. You sucked the sherbet up through a liquorice tube, then you ate the tube just as soon as you'd finished sneezing.

Having done all that, I returned to the game, won again, demanded another prize and was told I had already had one. This was injustice on a cosmic scale. I pursued my hostess like a bloodhound. Whenever she turned it was to see a plump little boy with his hand out. That I got another sherbet fountain in the end was due less to my legal case than to my doggedness. That I can remember the tone with which the mother finally conceded suggests perhaps the birth of self-awareness.

At the same party there was orange squash in thin glass tumblers. Used to chunkier tumblers or plastic ones, I bit the rim of the glass. It snapped and crunched between my teeth. I had fragments lying gaggingly on my tongue. I wanted to swallow and spit at the same time. I compromised by screaming. Mothers came running. One plucked glass from my mouth with tweezers while my own mother held my jaws open. I was back at Mr Fisher's.

Willingdon lies at the foot of the South Downs, a range of chalk hills with a skin of springy turf. For my mother the Downs were her mental salve, the place she went to throughout her life for a sense of wellbeing. When I was the last of her four children not yet at school, she would often take me for a snatched hour on the Downs, to clear, as she put it, the cobwebs. To this day the Downs are my template of countryside – windy, open, fresh.

I learned from my mother the names of the wild flowers, names as old as the language: lady's slipper, cuckoopint, campion, deadnettle, hawkbit, birdsfoot trefoil. Sometimes she'd take a flower home to confirm its identity. Her reference book graded plants for rarity, with the rarest having three stars. I yearned to find a three-star flower but never did better than two.

Then my father got a new job and we moved. We went twenty miles west of Eden, to the village of Hassocks, near Brighton, and a raw, new house on a raw, new housing estate.

Chapter 2

My mother's father died when I was seventeen. I'd always liked him. I went to see him in a hospice in Brighton. There was a television above the bed showing cricket highlights from Australia. Lillee and Thomson were terrifying the English batsmen.

Though Grandpop had no interest in cricket, he tried to say things about it because he knew I played, but he had cancer of the throat and there was almost no voice left. And coughs racked him. He'd been a twelve-stone man. Now he weighed six. He was hollowed out, skeletal, grey. He could get no food down. They gave him half-pints of Guinness to sip, decanted into a baby's plastic cup.

We watched the cricket for a bit, then he gestured to me to hand him a black book from a bedside drawer – his form book, in which he kept records of race horses, his only sporting interest. The pages were dense with neat notes. He wrote down the names of two horses, the times and places they were running, gave me £2 from the same bedside drawer and asked me to go lay a bet on each. I would need to hurry, he suggested. The bookmakers would be closing.

I had no doubt he was doing it as a kindness, but I was grateful for the excuse to leave. I thought of not placing the bet, of keeping the money. Perhaps he'd meant me to, but I was curious to enter a betting shop. I'd only ever looked through the doors at the little men and the television screen and the litter of paper and the fabulous fug of cigarette smoke. Nowhere on earth was smokier than a betting shop. I placed the bets.

Grandpop was born in 1895, about the same time as the first motor car. He never owned one. The hamlet of Isfield in Sussex where he was raised would have been like a Hardy novel: horses, carts, crops, candles, shepherds in smocks, Victoria on the throne and a horizon that stretched all the way to the next village. And he retained something of that rural patience, that unflustered submission to the seasons and the way things were.

He left school at twelve as everyone did and worked on a farm. Then the First World War gave him a chance to see the world. They sent him to East Africa, what is now Mozambique and Kenya, where he saw no fighting.

I have a few postcards he sent back, and the medals they gave him just for being there. He loved Africa, apparently, wanted to stay, but already, at the age of twenty, he was married and obliged. The chance to go anywhere never came again.

He did many things – tobacconist, railwayman, clock cleaner, nothing that ever paid much. He and his wife could not have children. They adopted my mother as a baby. She knew them as Ma and Pop.

Throughout my childhood we went to see them most weekends in their tiny dark front room in Eastbourne. They had an armchair each aligned to a little black and white television, where of a Saturday afternoon Pop would be watching the horses on *Grandstand* and smoking skinny roll-ups and Ma would be sucking mint imperials. A goldfinch hopped from perch to perch in a cage on the mantelpiece, its brilliance long since faded. I never heard it sing.

Pop would say little. Ma would issue a shrill torrent of complaint. Many years later my mother told me she was a cruel woman. Pop, however, she loved. They came over each Christmas Day and Pop would stand around being benign and deferring to everyone. He seemed to see the world with a kindly absence of expectation, which he would never dream of imposing on anyone else. He was modest and practical, and just once he took me fishing, on a stretch of beach somewhere near Eastbourne.

He had made his own rod and reel. The rod was bamboo, the eyes whipped on and the whole thing varnished to a gleam. The handle was of tightly wound cord. And the reel was a wooden centre-pin, turned on a lathe and dark with age and handling. It wound in oiled silence.

The tide was coming in. He paid out line and placed his baited hook in a rock pool just above the water's edge, then went back up the beach, stood the rod in a rod holder with a bell clipped to its tip, and went to sleep in a deckchair with his brown felt hat pulled over his eyes. In the thin brown suit he always wore – with braces and a collarless shirt – against the blue striped canvas, he looked like a dumped sack.

While he snoozed I played in the rock pools, each a temporary aquarium of darting fish fry, transparent shrimps, swaying strands of seaweed – a captive miniature world. There were alien anemones whose sprays of waving tentacles I was shy of, and little crabs whose claws I dreaded, crabs that scuttled unnervingly sideways, then shimmied down into the sand like settling skirts. I was wary, too, of the sea itself, its waves, its saltiness. As it crept back over the rocks I stayed well ahead of it, and went back up to Pop, who had woken and now sat with a finger crooked around the line just above the reel.

And without fuss he noted a knock on the line, took the rod from the holder, checked the feel of the line again, raised the rod tip and then reeled from the sea and up onto the beach a plaice, flapping wildly on the sand where I ran down to fetch it. Then he packed up fishing for the day.

When Ma died my mother found Pop a little flat to move into but almost as soon as he went there cancer got him, and my mother brought him to live with us. Us, by then, meant just her and me. I was in my last year at school.

Pop sat all day in what had been my father's armchair, a faux-luxurious leather beast that swivelled. Beside the chair he kept a little plastic bowl with a lid. Whenever he coughed, which was often, and paroxysmically, he would swivel the chair away, and spit a slither of thick and bloody phlegm into the bowl, then click the lid back on. Even in my self-absorbed adolescence I noted how hard he tried not to intrude.

Many evenings my mother would be out at her job on a hospital switchboard and she would leave instructions for me to cook dinner for Pop. But he would never let me, would insist that he'd eaten or wasn't hungry. And despite the fact that he was dying he mended the bathroom door.

It had always been warped. To lock it you had to lean a shoulder against it just above the handle. One day I came home from school to find the lock and handles removed, and a little bag of tools stashed by the towel rail: chisels, screwdrivers, a hand drill, their wooden handles worn smooth by use and polished by skin grease. The following day the tools had gone again and the door was reassembled, and the key now turned in the lock as sweetly as one could wish, at the bidding of just finger and thumb. And it did so for the following forty years, years when my mother occupied that house alone. And always, when I visited, to close the bathroom door was to remember Grandpop, kindly, patient, skilled, free of all resentment, a man who, had he had the opportunities, might have been remarkable.

The horses he bet on lost. I didn't go back to the hospice. He died before the test match had finished. If there was a funeral I didn't go. I don't think there's a grave, or any sort of memorial. S. F. V. Gurr, he was. S was for Sidney.

Chapter 3

My father was Gordon Bennett. I have no reason to believe he was the original, but it didn't help. He'd served as an engineer during the war and had been involved in building temporary runways in Normandy to support the troops advancing after D-Day, but I learned of this years after he had died. Only once to my memory did he mention the war. I'd asked him why he didn't put jam on a piece of bread and butter, and he said that for anyone who'd lived through the war bread and butter was a luxury.

He liked things clean, neat, conventional and English. If you'd asked him what he'd fought for he'd have thought it a dumb question. If you'd pressed him he'd have said Jevington Cricket Club. My father loved cricket, though he wasn't much good at it. He bowled slow-medium nothings and he batted a little. But it was the doing of it that pleased him and Jevington was where he did it.

Jevington lies in a cleft of the South Downs, a few miles out of Eastbourne. There's a single road through it, a few houses, a pub and a church. A gate just along from the pub gave access to a cricket field so steeply sloping that no one had ever been known to hit a six up the hill.

The field was rented for a shilling a year from the double-barrelled local landowner, a man of wealth and mystery who was never seen. Even in his absence he topped the class pyramid. From the middle classes there were a couple of local government officers like my father, a schoolteacher, a surveyor and a joyful freckled estate agent. The local publican played as well, though he had to leave the game at 6 pm to open the bar.

My heroes were of the working class. Prime among these was Mick Gates, the coalman, his forearms like blackened hams. He defined muscular manhood. He was the fast bowler and hitter of sixes into the wheat field. At the crease he leant his knee against the back of the bat. I did the same for years.

Jack Climpson seemed a thousand years old but was probably about thirty. He worked on the land and his head was a beard with two eyes in it, eyes that gleamed with slow kindness. He drove a prehistoric Land Rover and bowled round-arm off-breaks so slowly that you doubted the ball would arrive. Nothing could ever upset him. He seemed as immovable as the Downs. He had fathered two strong-limbed boys of about my age, and we romped and battled and climbed over him and his Land Rover as if both were features of the landscape. The boys spoke carefully and were infinitely braver than I.

At the foot of the field stood two wooden sheds painted white. One was the changing shed. It smelt of cobwebs and wood rot and leather and men. There was a piano in there with several keys still working. 'Please send your son outside,' said a visiting player to my father as I thumped those keys, 'I'm going to change my trousers.'

The other shed housed the mower and the pitch-marking apparatus and the wheeled device for painting a boundary line and all the rest of the simple mechanical gear associated with tending a cricket field, all of it lovely, smelling of whitewash and grass clippings and oil. And it was in this shed that the wives and girlfriends, with varying degrees of willingness, prepared and served the afternoon tea. For sixpence you got two sandwiches, a slice of home-made cake and a cup of tea, poured from a vast and dented pot.

The men's lavatory was the hedge; the women's a ditch beyond the hedge.

The roller stood in the long grass. It was two huge conjoined cylinders of metal, warmed by the sun, five foot tall and brown as the soil. It was fronted with shafts to which a horse could be harnessed but I only ever saw men shift it. Four or more of them would rock it in its cradle of sunk soil and yellowed grass, and then with a collective heave haul it over the lip and onto the field. Up and down the pitch they went and then back to beyond the boundary where it lived, for us kids to clamber on and feel the smoothed heat of the metal on the backs of our legs.

The cricket was rural, governed less by skill than by chance. Despite the rolling, the pitch was dicey, the scores low. The batting gloves had green rubber spikes on the fingers. The pads were thin. The bats were decades old and the colour of mahogany. The scoreboard was tin plates hung on three rows of nails. The top row, the innings total, rarely made use of the third nail.

Yet for me it was the original and best cricket, the archetypal game, and the men who played it are vivid to me still. Dougy Slade the publican, Freddie Feakins who sang and was funny, Arthur Langford the merry schoolmaster, Derek Hitchcock who was kind and whose combed-over hair dropped to his shoulder when he ran, the violinist with the Eastbourne symphony orchestra who loved the game but would not stop a moving ball, Jack Climpson, Mick Gates, Philip and Vivian Fowler.

Vivian was only seventeen or so, a local boy. Left-handed, long-nosed, graceful, he was clearly destined to go beyond Jevington. He once, to universal wonder, scored a fifty. Nobody scored fifty. Teams didn't score fifty. I begged to change my name to Vivian.

Dougy Slade's pub was the Eight Bells. All the players and wives trooped inside after the game while we boys sat on a tall flint wall overlooking a paddock of giant pigs. One of my nightmares was falling off into the mud and being eaten. But the fear was part of the thrill, straddling the crest of the wall, feeling on the inside of the thigh the cold glass of the shorn flint and the rough rub of the mortar. Every now and then in the twilight the door of the pub would open and emit a great sough of smoke and light and adult laughter and it seemed the most wonderful place in the world, the place you wanted to be.

I'd fall asleep in the car on the way home and be lifted out and dropped in the bath before bed and my sunburn would sting so as I entered the water that I'd scream. And my mother would swab my scarlet shoulders with calamine lotion on a wad of cotton wool. I haven't seen calamine lotion for half a century but if you opened a bottle now I'd know it by the smell.

Chapter 4

If I gave any thought to dogs in my first five years I don't remember it. Then my father came home with a puppy. I've since learned that my mother was appalled. Not because she didn't like puppies but because she knew it would fall to her to look after it, just as it fell to her to look after the house and the children. My father was nothing if not of his time. His job was to provide. He handed over the puppy in the same way as he handed over his salary. He'd done his bit.

The pup was a short-haired cream-coloured mongrel. Two years after it arrived I wrote a book. I've still got it. It is written in pencil, its subject is dogs and its title is 'Dogs'.

The first chapter of 'Dogs' is two pages long. It enumerates the virtues of short-haired cream-coloured mongrels and includes a photograph of one pasted beside the text. Chapter Two is one page long and consists of a poem copied from an anthology. Chapter Three is entitled 'Other Breeds' and is back to two pages in length but the handwriting gets consistently larger as it proceeds. By the bottom of the second page it's two words to a line. Then the book ends.

Just as my first book was about dogs, so my first ever newspaper column, thirty-five years later, was about dogs. But its title wasn't 'Dogs'. Its title was 'The Anagrams of God'. We don't change; we do get more pretentious.

The poem I included in the book was by Irene Rutherford McLeod, though I didn't credit her. Here's the first and best verse:

I'm a lean dog, a keen dog, a wild dog, and lone;
I'm a rough dog, a tough dog, hunting on my own;
I'm a bad dog, a mad dog, teasing silly sheep;
I love to sit and bay the moon, to keep fat souls from
sleep.

That I quoted it aged seven suggests that I saw in dogs then what I see in them now. They're wolves, and it still feels a privilege to have a wolf on the sofa, snoring beside me, a wolf whose jaws could crush the bones in my arm, but whose head lies heavy on my lap. And a privilege to see him running in his dreams and barking at some imagined quarry, and a privilege to calm his dreams by lightly laying a hand upon his chest. Attenborough travels thousands of miles to see nature in the raw. Owning a dog is cheaper and easier.

The cream-coloured mongrel was christened Rebel, which was apt. To a profoundly conventional household, a household that could not have been more middle-middle class, he brought a note of anarchy. Rebel destroyed stuff. He ate shoes. He ate coal. He dug where he shouldn't. He went where he shouldn't. He jumped fences or dug under them. He rolled in what stank. He once ran though a frosted glass window. He scrabbled at doors till his paws bled.

No one in the family had the least idea how to train a dog. After a couple of his more egregious crimes, my father dragged him out to the garage, dragged him cringing and fearful and bewildered, and beat him. I didn't dare to protest and had to run away so as not to hear the sound of the blows or the cries of the dog. And I remember thinking even then how unfair it was, how the dog would have no idea why he was being beaten. He would know only fear and pain.

But the beatings were few and they didn't break him. He was irrepressible, a joyous anarchist, a force of nature. Just as little children do, he found the world sufficient, loved what was there. And I loved him, of course. And one cost of love is pain. I remember most the moments of horror.

Loud noises terrified him. During thunderstorms I would withdraw with him into the cupboard under the stairs where there were old jackets, and the ironing board, and unused pots, and the vacuum cleaner, and I'd sit with my arm around him in the darkness and at every peal of thunder he'd thrum like a tuning fork, the shudder filling his body, and he'd squirm and whimper, his ears flattened, his whole posture pitiful, and I would feel the lover's impotence to take the pain onto myself.

Fireworks were an especial trial. Back then every corner shop sold them for a month or more before the fifth of November and every boy had a pocketful of bangers that rang out in the evening like small-arms fire. Rebel lived the month in terror. One Bonfire Night he jumped the garden fence. My father drove us around to look for him, but without success. Rebel limped back at dawn, his right flank bruised and bleeding, seemingly having been struck by a car. We smeared his wounds with ointment. He licked it off and in the manner of dogs lay down to get better. Never once in his long life did he go to the vet.

But he did go to kennels. When we went on summer holiday my father took him to Woodside Kennels.

Rebel knew what was coming and he fought all the way, sinking his heels in, writhing to slip his collar, battling with every sinew of his self. For three weeks at the kennels he would pine. He ate nothing. On holiday I was sufficiently selfish to forget about him, but the moment we got back I would run to Woodside to fetch him and he would explode from the kennels, dowdy and lustreless, his ribs showing, but frantic, unstoppable with happiness, running-in-circles happy. He made me cry.

At Jevington one Saturday I opened the boot of the car to let him out but his lead was looped around the wing nut that clamped the spare wheel in place. As he jumped down, the lead pulled him up short of the ground and twisted him around and he was arched on his back over the sill and his collar was throttling him. And I can see now his paws wildly thrashing the air and the terror in his eyes and I can hear the gurgle of asphyxiation. I tried to unhitch the lead but was too weak and I was watching the dog die and then my father seized him and lifted him back into the boot and unclipped the lead and Rebel shook himself and jumped down and was whole and happy on the instant. That was sixty years ago. It remains more vivid than this morning.

But Rebel fought. He would erupt from the dog I loved into a beast who was all teeth and noise and violence.

And the dogs he started fights with were always bigger than him and they did him terrible damage. High on the South Downs one sunny afternoon an Airedale terrier pinned him to the ground and sank teeth into his head an inch from his eye. In Adastra Park a German shepherd latched onto his throat and would have killed him had not the owner hauled it off. And in the stream at the bottom of Chancellors Park he took on a pair of boxers, and he never stood a chance. I had been walking him alone and the boxers had no owner and I stood motionless and terrified on the bank above as they pinned him underwater and I could see him drowning. And then miraculously they'd had enough, had made their point, and let him go and walked away, and he came up gasping but alive, and shook himself and went back for more. Again the nightmare stays with me. Though it was not the boxers' fault, I still don't trust the breed, will often, at the sight of one, feel an involuntary shiver of memory.

Rebel died when I was at university. He'd outlived the family he'd grown up with. My father was dead, my brothers and sister and I had long since gone. Only my mother was left at home. Years later she told me how much she had come to depend on Rebel as a confidant. What she couldn't tell her husband or her children, she told the dog, in that red-tiled kitchen where he hung around for scraps, or on the cheap 1960s sofa where they had an end each.

What my mother did with Rebel's corpse I don't know. There's no grave I know of, nor any urn. But she never forgot him, would always lavish love on any dog that resembled him.

And he was immortalised on the kitchen door. If in 2015 the ambulance men had glanced up as they were wheeling my ninety-two-year-old mother out through that door, never to return, they might have noticed, just above the handle, and smoothed over by several coats of paint, the marks of his scrabbling claws scored deep into the wood.

Chapter 5

I have just one photograph from Willingdon. My father took it. It shows my mother standing in the front garden with her daughter and three sons. Star of the show is a ten-pound pike that my brother Nigel is holding by the gills. My sister Nicola does not seem to want anything to do with the event, my brother Simon is looking coy, and I, at the age of maybe four, am holding onto my mother's skirt looking happy and fat. My nickname within the family was Podge.

Nigel was ten years older, my parents' first child. Like me he had vivid red hair. Unlike me he was tall, skinny, angular. And from as far back as I can remember he took me fishing.

Why he should go fishing with his kid brother rather than his contemporaries I didn't question at the time. As I look back now, he seems to have had no gift for friendship. But he did for fishing. He had a nose for fish.

He thought like a fish. Even when I was in my teens, and he was already on his way to being a drunk, we would fish side by side with identical tackle and he would catch five fish to my one. When fishing he was intent, benign, absorbed, happy. When not fishing he was a thwarted mess.

All fishing was good to him. He took me to the sluggish lowland rivers of the Weald, the Cuckmere, the Adur. He took me to ponds out the back of farms where he knew there were tench or carp, to a stream near Plumpton where we poached four-ounce trout by trotting worms and I was terrified of being caught and imprisoned; and once he took me to fish for pike. It was on the marshes behind Pevensey in crunching frozen winter, with ice on the edges of the slow streams and the landscape brown and grey against a sky the colour of elephant skin. He gave me a plug to fish with, a little hinged lure set with treble hooks, that on retrieval writhed and bobbed across the surface of the water like an improbably wounded fish. And on my third or fourth cast a pike drifted in behind the plug, bulging the water, its dorsal fin breaking into air, and it followed the plug as I wound it towards me and I could barely breathe with the excitement and the fear, could barely force myself to keep winding the reel, to keep the plug moving, and I wound it almost to the bank with the pike moving in behind, then it caught sight of me and swirled and was gone. And I was shaking too much to cast again immediately, was weak, drained.

My brother's creel was a heavy wicker box with a canvas strap. Inside it, among all the pleasing tackle that fishing generates, was a spring-loaded gag. It consisted of a pair of metal arms with backward-facing barbs on their tips. A clip held the arms together. Release it and they sprang apart. Their function was to hold a pike's jaws open while you extracted the hook. That gag was all you needed to know about pike.

We fished the sea as well. Brighton had two piers, striding out towards France on legs of Victorian ironwork. In summer they offered ooh-la-la naughtiness, and ghost trains and halls of mirrors. But Brighton was fading as a resort. The beach had never been sandy. The weather had never been Spanish. The glamour had only ever been tat. And the piers were already shabby and peeling. In winter fishermen took them over.

The Palace Pier in January was bracingly austere. A stout timber and glass partition ran the length of it like a spine, creating leeward and windward. Windward could be uninhabitable, with a gale you could lean on, head down into it against the nails of flung spray, or ballooning along with it, laughing at your moon-strides, cheeks numb, hair smacking like snakes, too loud to hear your own bellow, and then you would let yourself be blown through a gap in the partition and you were suddenly leeward in silence and calm, and you'd laugh.

The leeward rail would be lined with rods, a phalanx of them, propped at an angle, nodding in unison as a wave leant on the lines and then let them go. Some men pinned bells to the rod to warn of bites, but most stood watching their rod tips or held a finger against the line as if taking a pulse. In the lee of the partition lay their little scatter of stuff: a creel or tackle box, a folding chair, a roll of stained newspaper holding a dozen lug worms, a fishmonger's herring half-butchered for bait, the long rusting forensic-evidence knife that did the butchering, a dented Thermos flask. On a winter Saturday there could be several hundred of us, exclusively men and boys, with the lazy sub-Cockney accent of the south-east.

And we'd own that leeward side. Any promenadist, any non-fishing constitutional-taker, would be intimidated by the smell of bait and fish-flesh scored into the timbers, and by the rough-dressed masculinity of it all, like a gold-rush town. And especially by the casting.

To cast you stood at the rail with your rod held above and behind you, a spiked lead weight and several baited hooks dangling from the tip, and then you lurched the whole assembly up and forward, making the rod bend to fling the weight and bait as far as possible from the pier. Good casters could do sixty yards or more, though there was no virtue in distance. The fish were as likely, more likely even, to be pecking around the piles of the pier beneath us. But casting was the theatre of manhood.

The trick of it lay in releasing the line at the right moment to let the tackle fly. Release too early and the weight and hooks would soar straight up into the air before coming down humiliatingly close to the pier or, worse still, and terrifyingly, on the pier itself. Release too late and the weight would clang into the metal rail and wrap itself around.

Everyone had a casting horror story, of hooks slicing open a cheek, or flipping an eyeball out to sea. I doubted them all and passed them on with relish. The worst I saw was a youth hooked by the tail of his parka. Neither he nor the parka flew out to sea but the force of the cast was enough to wrench him around. 'Fuck,' he screamed with the shock of it, and then as the fear drained and he examined the hooked tail of his coat, as if suddenly exhausted, 'Fucking hell.'

Men watched each other cast in silent judgment. When you got it right, when the line went singing off the spool of the multiplier reel, and when, as the bait struck the water, you stopped the reel from overspinning by braking it with your thumb, and you propped your rod against the rail and felt the line for tautness, and admired your rod tip silhouetted against the sky, and you drank Bovril from the plastic top of the flask, then you felt that you belonged to a fraternity, and there was no better way to spend a winter Sunday, godless, wind-ravaged, raw and predatory. And with your finger on the stretch of line between the reel and the first eye, alert for the knock of a living creature, you could look back to the steep stone beach and the line of whitewashed Edwardian hotels and the raised promenade with its scatter of head-scarved winter walkers, and think 'landlubbers'.

Only once in all the time I fished from the pier did the waters teem. One summer a vast shoal of mackerel blew in and the sea went from barren to fecund in half an hour. Anyone could catch fish and anyone did. Men and boys hauled them up two, three, four at a time, ripping them from the hooks and leaving them to flap to death on the boards of the pier while they dropped the line back in for more. We caught them by the dozen, by the hundred, caught them for no reason, caught them not to eat or to give away, but just to catch them, a jackpot of fish, a sort of blue-green compensation for the fishless days.

For in truth that part of the English Channel seemed used up, stripped of life, even then, in the 1960s, when the world in general seemed limitlessly abundant. Too many ships had plied that water, too many battles had been fought on it, too many nets hauled through it, too much waste pumped into it, and what was left was a squalid vestige of an aquatic world, a grim parody of the teeming transparent seas where Jacques Cousteau went diving on the telly.

The most telling thing about the paltry fish we generally caught was that you often didn't know you'd hooked them. A suggestion of a bite, a rattle on the rod tip, a pulse sensed on the line and you picked up your rod and cocked your head, intent on what was happening on the unseen sea bed, and if you convinced yourself that there was action down there in the darkness you struck, then wound it in. No arching rod, no screaming reel, no *Old Man and the Sea* communion with a fish, just winding it in till the four ounces of lead and a tangle of hooks rose from the churning water and you had perhaps a one-pound ling, or maybe a spider crab that clung on for half the haul to the railing, then let go and fell back into the sea, or, more likely, nothing.

Nevertheless I loved it, loved it from the first time Nigel took me at the age of six or so. There had to be the chance of fish, the necessary hope, but it was the doing of it that thrilled me, the scouring, rinsing nature of the pier in winter that kept me coming back to the line of men and rods throughout my youth. The men smoked, all of them, Embassy or No. 6, and they swore, and their clothes were black or brown or simply dark, and the deck was smeared with bait and guts, and if you looked down through the gaps between the wooden boards you could see the sea swirling beneath you.

And then in adolescence came the night fishing, whole nights on the shingle beach, casting out into the breakers, propping the rod vertical and then standing beside it to watch the tip in silhouette against the scudding clouds. Moonlight on the sea was a form of magic, and for noise there was only the ceaseless suck and hiss of the shingle, and all of it enlivened by the transgressive sense of being up and fishing at three in the morning when all the world was asleep. And watching dawn lighten the sky by degrees and when finally the milk floats and bread vans and the first buses started up along the seafront, to pack up the gear and head back up the beach, the stones sinking beneath your feet like the sands of the desert, to the transport café on the front, its windows steamed with frying, and to have eggs, bacon, sausage and fried bread, with a mug of tea you could trot a mouse on.

In my youth I only ever saw three fish of substance hooked. One was a cod of twenty pounds, a grey-brown huge-headed magnificence, caught near the ghost train by a man who looked like the elder Steptoe. The news of his catch spread the length of the pier and every fisherman that afternoon went to see it, to stand mute and reverent before it. The following week Steptoe and his fish appeared on an inside page of *Angling Times* and I felt that I had touched the Happy Isles and seen the great Achilles, whom we knew.

And then there were the conger eels. The first was hooked by a kid of ten on a stout little boat rod just like mine. A crowd gathered and craned over the railing and men helped the boy to wind his reel against what seemed like some monstrous force until a great grey head broke the surface, an ancient head, reptilian, grizzled, and from its jaw there hung a dozen scraps of fishing line, the hooks and lures embedded in its cheeks and lips, enfleshed, grown over, and the lines were like whiskers.

The great fish seemed inert until someone lowered a drop net, and then it writhed, once, a single spasm of the flesh, and the line snapped like cotton and the fish sank back down into the dishwash-coloured sea and the kid let out a wail. And I remember feeling disappointed but also relieved, for I had been scared.

It was years later that I saw the other conger eel, this one on Newhaven breakwater, but that story can wait, because by then I was on the other side of puberty, and everything had changed.

Chapter 6

Breakfast some time in 1964. There was always a cooked breakfast – sometimes bacon and fried bread, gleaming with fat and snappable, but more often beans on toast. The beans were Crosse & Blackwell, all other brands being deemed common.

We ate at the dining room table: my mother at the kitchen end so she could fetch and serve, my father at the window end and children on the sides. It was like one of those line drawings of the time, advertising middle-class contentment: mother in a dress and apron, father in collar and tie, children scrubbed and uniformed for school, a paradigm of post-war prosperity and orthodoxy, even to the light, sleek, insubstantial furniture. Pan out and the picture became even more of its time, with the brand-new estate, detached brick houses each with a garage and an indoor bathroom, and an extra toilet downstairs and a fenced back garden. It was the epitome of the post-war boom, of 'you never had it so good'.

But Nigel had not come down for breakfast. He was seventeen by now. He had grown his hair into a bouffant ginger mess. And his body had struck out suddenly to over six foot of height, and he had a bedroom to himself with a record player, the standard box on legs that played the The Animals and The Kinks. All of the above, every molecule of it, antagonised my father, because he couldn't understand it – not the hair, not the music, not the private bedroom, not even the extraordinary height of his son, he being only five foot seven. He did not understand what he had spawned. His own adolescence had been during the Depression, when teenageship was a luxury the world could not yet afford.

Nigel and my father had skirmished many times and were clearly heading for the main event. All it needed was a spark. And failing to get up in the morning was exactly that, for it enshrined the whole of my father's case, that my brother was spoilt, ungrateful, selfish, rude, an unclean thing. I doubt he had ever said any of those words, or even gone so far as to form them in his mind, but he didn't need to. He knew action was needed, and he was not one to back down from conflict.

My mother, sniffing the wind, anxious to placate, had called upstairs. And now she sent me, aged seven. I was always the one sent, the other redhead, and the only member of the family who had any influence on Nigel. But I dreaded the mission. Friction was brewing and friction made me feel sick, unable to swallow food, to think of other things, to smile.

My brother's room smelt of socks and sweat and excretions. He lay foetally, face to the wall, the sheets and blankets a twisted mess. He had demons. He didn't sleep in a bed so much as wrestle with it. His left shoulder was exposed above the bedclothes, the skin garlic white. I laid a hand on it. It was clammy.

'Bloggs,' I said. It was what we called each other when fishing. I don't know why. 'Bloggs.'

He struggled all his life with the world's official rhythm. He rarely slept before three in the morning. If left alone he'd sleep till three in the afternoon.

'Bloggs,' I said again, and with visible effort he managed to mutter that he was coming. But you could sense sleep like a set of hands pulling him back under. I urged him again, and he promised he was on his way.

'He's on his way,' I said back at the breakfast table and the tension rose a notch and the meal went on in silence.

When he appeared at the dining room door some minutes later he had pulled on trousers and a shirt. No socks and the shirt hung loose about his waist. His hair was a haystack, his face still folded with sleep.

My father was not an angry man or a violent one, but he had a temper born of a sense of propriety and when it blew, it blew. It blew now. He pushed his chair back and stood and my brother saw what was coming and turned away and my father swung a kick at his backside and another and another, kicks for being a canker and a threat of chaos in a right and proper home. And my brother whimpered and hunched and fled from the room pursued by my father, still swinging his righteous kicks.

Not long after that, Nigel left school and then home. I suspect my mother of engineering the move because my father and he just couldn't share a house. Nigel went to some college to study town planning. Why town planning I have no idea. It would be hard to think of a course of study to which he was less suited.

There was a television programme called 'Out of Town' in which Jack Hargreaves demonstrated rural skills: how to make an eel trap, skin a rabbit, fish for carp, all of which was pleasing stuff. But better even than the content was the manner. He smoked a pipe that he would lay aside as the programme began and then he would speak in a gentle unhurried voice, as one who harboured no ambition, who was content with the way of the world and his place within it. No doubt there was an element of performance to it all but the man seemed as relaxed as the landscape, as languid as the rivers we fished. Jack Hargreaves presented a world in which my brother could live.

Nigel should have been a water bailiff, someone who managed a stretch of river for a fishing club. He often spoke of it but he did nothing to bring it about. He had demons, but they fell silent in the countryside. When he was fishing or stalking the frozen fields with a shotgun, he was at ease with himself, absorbed and fully alive. He was not, and never would be, a town planner.

To complete the qualification he had to write a dissertation on some planning matter. For years my mother would speak of the dissertation as the final hurdle that stood between her troubled son and a better life. It was a hurdle he never jumped. Though he did eventually go to work for Brighton Borough Council, he was always in the wrong business.

A couple of years after he left home he came to the house late one night when everyone was asleep and woke me and led me downstairs to meet his girlfriend. Mary sat beside me on the sofa and I showed her a bird book

I'd been given for my birthday. As far as I know Mary was the only girlfriend he ever had. They married ten years later, in a registry office. I was best man. There were plastic flowers on the filing cabinet and a reception at a pub in Ditchling.

But Nigel was already sliding into drink. He bought the trappings of a Jack Hargreaves world – a battered Land Rover, a black lab called Sam, guns, rods, a hen coop, even a ferret from Lewes market where there were still shepherds in smocks – but the reality of his work in the planning department depressed him. To pay for his drinking he took backhanders from cowboy builders. He found me summer jobs with them when I was at university. In the end he was suspended from work, pending an investigation into corruption. He borrowed money wherever he could, stole from my mother, drank to oblivion, and then Mary left him, taking their two daughters.

In his forties he fetched up on an oil rig in the North Sea, where he suffered an embolism of the brain and was airlifted to a hospital in Norwich. My mother went to see him, despite their estrangement, and found her eldest son writhing on the bed, oblivious and shouting a torrent of obscenities. He died within days.

I flew back from New Zealand for the burial, in the graveyard of a country church overlooking the Weald.

From the wicket gate you could see a little river shining silver. There was no service, no vicar, just six gloomy men hired by the undertaker to carry the coffin from the hearse to the grave. The mourners were his mother, his estranged wife, his three siblings and a representative from the oil company who had never met him.

We stood around as the coffin was lowered. Nothing was said. My mother threw in a handful of soil. And we left.

Chapter 7

I ached to go to school, not because I was keen to learn, nor yet because I thought I would be happy there, but because it was the next thing. Always too eager for the future, wrote Larkin.

School was easy. My mother had taught me to read and write long before I got there. I remember nothing of the lessons taught, only of the oddity of other kids. In Mrs Coghlin's class I was sat next to a chunky little boy called Adam. When we were doing drawing, his idea of fun was to lob a scrunched-up piece of paper onto the floor in the vague direction of Mrs Coghlin. He would then run after it, sink to his knees, slide across the polished parquet and collect the paper with a view to carrying on sliding until he came to rest against Mrs Coghlin's ankles. He would then sneak a look up her skirt. It was the best thing ever, he said. He urged me to have a go. We were five years old.

I went on through twelve years of schooling with Adam. By the age of thirteen he was collecting sexual paraphernalia in the way the rest of us collected stamps. He boasted of having everything from condoms to pornography via sanitary towels and vibrators. At fifteen, when he was on a train to school on which there happened to be a party of Swedish girls, his erection burst through the cloth of his school trousers like the monster in *Alien*. No doubt the cloth had been weakened by repeated stress but it was still appallingly impressive. Most remarkable to me, however, was his utter lack of shame, indeed his delight. He showed off the flap of cloth to anyone who'd look. At sixteen he left school, became a mechanic and ran a repair shop in rural Sussex for a while but the call of his nature proved irresistible. When last I heard, he was running a chain of dance clubs in Thailand.

At Hassocks County Infant School we put chairs on tables at the end of the day and mumbled a prayer with our eyes shut. Like all the religious elements of my schooling this was a husk, bereft of substance or significance. Indeed throughout my education no one at all, neither teaching nor taught, professed any religious belief. It was a lucky time and place.

During one end-of-schoolday blessing Steven Hawkins threw up. Through eyes screwed to slits I watched the stew we'd had for lunch gush from his mouth. It seemed unaltered. And in the mind's eye, which, as Wordsworth reminds us, is the bliss of memory, I can still see, in perfect detail, more than half a century later, a greyish cube of beef emerging from his left nostril like an animal squeezing out of a too-small burrow.

The playground was sunk below the level of the high street so mothers could stand at the railings and watch their offspring playing like kittens in a pet-shop tank. Some mothers came every playtime. I was grateful, even at five, that mine didn't. Betrayal starts early. By the age of six on the way to school I would feign a reason to run ahead of my mother or lag behind. I knew that she knew what I was doing and why, and I also knew that it must have hurt.

The school was impeccably co-educational. The girls were taught nothing that the boys weren't and vice versa. But outside the classroom we imposed our own instinctive sexual apartheid. In the playground girls played mysterious games of make-believe that seemed to involve a lot of sitting with heads close together, but that was all we boys knew. Our games had different names – cops and robbers, cowboys and Indians – but were all the same in essence, simply huge and violent games of 'it'. To recruit others for a game you draped your arms over another boy's shoulders and began a rhythmic chant of 'Join on, cowboys and Indians'. What happened next was educative.

If you failed to recruit others in the first few moments you became a pariah. Your bid was doomed. There was no point in continuing. But if you succeeded in getting others to join on, if the line of linked bodies began to grow, it suddenly became the only game in town and you knew the dizziness of popularity. Moreover you were now at the centre of a line of perhaps thirty boys, each with his arms over the shoulders of the boy on either side, and the whole thing was moving around the playground like some ever-growing drift net. Girls squealed and ran. And positioned in the centre you could learn a lot about physics.

Simply by standing still and exerting a rotational movement you could cause the whole line to begin spinning like the Crab Nebula, with half the line going forwards, the other half backwards and with those near the centre doing no more than taking a few steps while those on the outer margins had to run screaming to keep up before centrifugal force broke their bonds and flung them against the brick wall of the air-raid shelter. Once, when flung against the wall myself, I burst into tears and ran wailing to Mrs Coghlin, as if drawn by some irresistible magnet. I sank my face into the rough tweed of her skirt and clamped my arms around her thighs and wailed like a professional mourner while registering only too consciously that Mrs Coghlin wasn't my mother and yet her skirt and thighs were every bit as consolatory.

After Hassocks County Infant School came Hassocks County Primary School, half a mile away in Dale Avenue. Within a year of my arrival the school changed its name to The Windmills, the justification being a pair of nineteenth-century windmills, Jack and Jill, on the crest of the South Downs. The windmills were five miles away. They didn't work. They weren't visible from most of the classroom windows. The school had nothing to do with them. We were never taken to see them. And yet suddenly we were named after them. Even at the age of seven I was irked by this exercise in branding, this verbal falsehood. But I still managed to have a good time.

At primary school our games became more violent. Pile-on involved any number of boys circling each other like so many sharks, waiting for a moment of inattention. The idea was to tackle another to the ground with a cry of 'Pile on', whereupon everyone flung themselves onto the victim until the squirming pile was four or five bodies deep and screams were coming from its core. Satisfied, we would all peel off and begin circling again.

The ideal victim was someone who didn't know he was playing. Someone such as, say, Andrew Towers, a studious boy who was minding his own business when suddenly tackled and smothered. When we all stood up again, Andrew Towers didn't. Nor did he speak. He just lay. Mr King came running across the playground, scooped him up and ran into the school with the boy draped limp in his arms, while we who had flung ourselves on top of him melted away. That afternoon Mr Bishop, the headmaster, who had eyebrows like small mice, and eyes so sunken they were lost in the gloom, summoned an emergency assembly at which he announced that Andrew Towers had stopped breathing and almost died and that the game of pile-on was banned in perpetuity. I was disappointed by the ban but thrilled by the proximity to death. Andrew Towers gained an enviable lustre.

We did graver damage to Vanessa Butler. She was a small quiet girl with dry hands and blue-rimmed glasses. We decided, for no reason other than the pleasure of persecution, that she smelt. We further decided – and the we, here, is a true collective noun, the whole of our class, both girls and boys, like a colony of ants acting as a single organism – that the reason she smelt was a highly contagious disease called Butler Bugs. So, if

Vanessa Butler came near, you had to mime injecting yourself in the arm with a prophylactic vaccine. You completed the charm by saying 'Injection'.

The result was an ostracism so complete that she spent weeks skulking around the edge of the playground and sitting on her own in class. That Vanessa Butler didn't go mad was due to the mid-term arrival in our class of Tina Jones. Tina Jones befriended Vanessa Butler. They became inseparable.

Tina was a big girl in a thin dress. In our utterly Anglo-Saxon corner of England her eyes were abnormally large and dark, though she kept them down-turned from shyness. Despite her size, she spoke in a whisper and never in class. Of course by befriending Vanessa Butler she was fatally infected with Butler Bugs, but then she was already a pariah. For Tina Jones was a gypsy.

Gypsies or gyppos were the only aliens in Hassocks, the only obvious outsiders. I feared and loathed them and wanted them cleared away, gone, banished. This was partly because they had parked their caravans between me and the reservoir overflow where I went fishing with Philip Dodds. But it was mainly because they were different. You can trace every war, every genocide, back to childish instinct.

That I remember our cruelty towards Vanessa Butler suggests that I knew in my bones it was wrong. But I was happy with it at the time. In *Lord of the Flies* I'd have laughed at the smashing of Piggy's glasses and I'd have helped to kill Simon.

Chapter 8

When Mr Bishop called the emergency assembly we sat cross-legged on the wooden floor of the hall. I found this hard because my legs were short and fat. I despaired of those legs early. Sitting on the lavatory, I would stare at the flattened mass of my thighs and sigh. I knew the thighs I wanted. They were Nick Hudson's.

Nick Hudson was a friend of my brother Simon. He was two years older than me and I considered him an ideal form, the way a boy should look. He was blond, angular of face, impertinent of manner and when he wore football shorts the cloth flapped in the breeze like a flag on a flagstaff because of those slim thighs. Nick Hudson became the template for the friends I made at primary school. I got on all right with most kids but I already and wordlessly felt the pull of beauty.

My best friends were Mike Mitchell and Dave Collier. Both were skinny and blond. Mike Mitchell in particular had the sort of Bubbles looks that sent mothers weak at the knees. But both had a further quality that I instinctively cleaved to, which was daring, an urge to mischief. They might look like David Copperfield, but they were the Artful Dodger. Mike, in particular, had a streak of raw violence that both thrilled and appalled me and made him the most feared opponent in the game of pug.

Pug happened at the lower end of Adastra Park where a stream had run through the Wealden clay for centuries and worn a canyon identical to its Grand equivalent in Arizona in every way except scale. Its sheer cliffs cut through strata and writhed with the water's course, but were nowhere more than two yards tall. In summer the streambed was more mud than running water.

Pug had no rules except violence. The aim was to maim. To play you needed a supple stick, hazel or similar, to the thin end of which you attached a gob of clay. Thus armed, you stalked the canyon. The idea was sneak up on others and fire the gob of clay at them, using the stick as a sort of sling. Often the clay would fall impotently in the backswing, but if you got it right it went with the speed of a bullet and would raise a welt like a small volcanic crater. Especially if, as was common, the mud pellet had been wrapped lovingly around a small stone for ballast. That none of us lost an eye you can put down to the god who looks after small boys playing rough games and drunks who mean well.

There were no teams in pug. You formed guerrilla bands, raiding parties that would sneak up on a lone victim and subject him to a sudden and glorious hail of fire. But every allegiance was transactional and temporary. Pug was an object lesson in fear, violence and perfidy. And it could go on delightfully all afternoon.

But however violent and cruel the game might be, to Mike Mitchell it could seem tame. Just as Hitler felt the need to open an eastern front, so Mike chose to expand the theatre of war.

On the far side of the stream lay Adastra Avenue. It consisted of a row of bungalows and front gardens so psychotically neat that just to walk past them was to feel a sense of stifling oppression. In its silence, order, conformity, its implicit fear, Adastra Avenue and others like it served as a warning to us all. Get out of Hassocks or this will be your lot. Though I have recently learned that, even while we were charging up and down the streambed armed with pug, William Plomer, a South African poet who lived with a man in Japan, saw Berlin in the 1930s, knew Gide, was friends with Auden and spoke at Ian Fleming's funeral (though that is not necessarily an accolade), lived at number 43 Adastra Avenue. How, I can't tell you.

Anyway, a householder who emphatically wasn't William Plomer was pushing a little mechanical mower back and forth across his scrap of lawn. This was separated from the pavement by a low and looping chain-link fence that had defeat written into its DNA. As a concession to the weekend, the householder had removed his tie. Mike Mitchell's angel face popped up over the lip of the streambed like one of those guardian meerkats.

It is hard to imagine a greater infraction of the suburban peace of Adastra Avenue than the sound of breaking glass. The man at the lawnmower, who would never know that he, rather than his window, had been the actual target of Mike Mitchell's attack, wheeled around with an expression that could have modelled for Munch. It took him less than a moment to work out where the missile had come from and he was already running towards us. My last glimpse of Mike as I took off in terror was of him cackling maniacally even as he reloaded. I avoided the stream and Adastra Avenue for days, fearing the authorities. I had mental images of tracker dogs and plaster casts of footprints in the streambed. Mike didn't of course. He moved merrily on to whatever transgression the next day would bring with the sort of insouciance that I have envied all my life.

Philip Dodds was the only boy I knew who fished. He was an ectomorph, a kid so skinny that bright light shone through him. His arms and legs were sticks, his head a skull tautly wrapped in skin. He wore the wire-framed spectacles we knew as National Health glasses. And he was gawky with it, jerky of movement, as if his muscles were stretched too tight and thin, like rubber bands, causing his limbs to move with suddenness. Despite all this, Philip Dodds was a grinner, an enthusiast. Propose a game, a plan, a fishing trip and he'd gush his support, constantly eager. Our best fishing spot was the reservoir overflow, but to get there we had to bike past the gypsies.

They lived in caravans on either side of Lodge Lane. The ground around them was mud, littered with broken cars, bikes, prams. Their dogs had ribs like toast racks and were tied to the caravans by old ropes or electrical flex. The children had black eyes and dirt around their mouths. The women looked worn and bitter and wore head-scarves, and the men had pot bellies and sinewy arms and skin the colour of nuts. And as we cycled past, all pink and keen and advertisement-clean, they eyed us, it seemed to me, with malice. Disorder, poverty, dirt, these had been swept out of my life before I arrived, but here they were on either side of Lodge Lane. I hid my fear from Philip Dodds, and I'm not sure that he felt anything similar. It was that sunniness of his, that gauche irrepressible merriment.

Beyond the gypsies it was just a quick pedal down a cart track to ditch our bikes by the gate, then run down through the grass to the reservoir overflow. The reservoir itself was steeply banked and fenced around with metal spikes, but below one end lay a pond that was home to a thousand stunted, interbred roach and rudd and bream and dace that competed to be caught. A willow tree grew out over the water at a spastic angle. Stretched out on one of its limbs with rod in hand you could watch the ephemeral shades of tiny fish besiege your breaded hook, pecking and battering it until bits fell off and it was small enough for one of their number to take it whole. At the end of the afternoon we would haul out a keepnet of perhaps twenty scraps of silver fish flesh, arching and flipping on the grass before we tipped them back.

There were other fish too, on the far side of the pond, the shadier side where the water was deeper and darker. Here lay the carp, unthinkable monsters of three, maybe four pounds. Sometimes we'd hear one suck at the surface, or slap down on it as it flopped beyond the bulrushes. These fish were the fish of legend, and we would make elaborate plans to catch one, and Philip Dodds would grin his grin that stretched his lips back from all his teeth at once so he looked like a preserved and shrunken head, and he'd twitch with the excitement. Maybe his faith in the world was such that he really did believe we could haul one of these monsters from the deeps. I never did.

One Sunday afternoon we heard the slurp of a carp on the far side of the bulrushes and Philip announced that he was going around to fish for it, and he crossed the little concrete weir and disappeared from view. It was not long after that I heard a sort of thwarted cry. I wanted to call out but I was scared to do so, and then there came a laugh and it wasn't Philip Dodds' laugh.

I ducked and hid, heard more laughter and two boys I didn't know came into view on the slope above the pond, not gypsy boys, but older than us, walking one in front of Philip Dodds and one behind, like slave traders. Each held one end of a rope that was looped around Philip Dodds' neck. They were walking him up the hill towards a copse and he was silent and pale and not grinning and he had never looked thinner.

They were going to lynch him. They were going to lob the rope over a branch and haul him high, the bone-thin, bespectacled Philip Dodds. He'd be easy to haul up. But it wasn't what they were going to do to him that appalled me, so much as what they were already doing, what they had already done. That rope around the throat, rubbing fibrous against his skin, and the laugh that came with it, the pleasure in the cruelty, in the hopelessness of his position, that was the horror of it. When they crested the ridge and went out of sight, I grabbed my rod and ran.

There was nothing I could have done against these bigger stronger boys, and it didn't cross my mind to try. I ran not to fetch help nor even to save my own skin. I ran to put distance between myself and this violence. I climbed the gate and pulled my bike from the hedge and biked for home and I cried as I biked. But I didn't cry at home. I didn't tell, couldn't tell, couldn't breathe a word of such deeds in our neat suburban home. I couldn't tell my mother or brothers that boys had slung a rope around Philip Dodds' neck and marched him off to hang. I just couldn't.

The police were not at school on Monday. Philip Dodds was. He seemed as cheerful and gawky as ever. I didn't let on that I'd seen what happened and he said nothing about it. Perhaps he was already used to being the victim. Perhaps he'd seen it all by the age of eight, knew all about the cruelty of some and the cowardice of others.

Philip Dodds and I went on to the same secondary school, but our social paths diverged and we rarely had anything much to do with each other. He remained one of the world's nice guys, though I have no doubt he would often have been bullied. There was something about his skinny innocence, his lack of cynicism, that would arouse a bully's cruelty.

Aged fourteen or so I was keeping goal in a house football match against a team that included Philip Dodds. He played football as he did everything, with happy energy. But he was so skinny that he was easily muscled off the ball. It was raining. Footballs then were made of heavy leather with a laced vent. Heading such a ball, even when dry, was an act of courage. Heading it wet was like heading a sandbag.

On this sodden afternoon, the ball was centred across my goal, and rising improbably to meet it at the far post was Philip Dodds. He could not have timed his run better. Perhaps eight yards from goal he leapt high above the defence, hung seemingly suspended a moment in mid-air, his body coiled in the shape of a seahorse, then he thrust his neck forward, met the ball square on his forehead and headed it into the top right-hand corner of the net. It was a freakishly beautiful goal. And it's my last memory of Philip Dodds.

Though after a few minutes research on the internet I have just found the minutes of a meeting of the Mental Health Foundation for the area we were brought up in. It regrets the sudden and unexpected death, at home, of a Philip Dodds, who had been for several years the patient representative on the board.

Chapter 9

My first memory of Adastra Park is cricket with my father on a summer evening. I don't think I ever saw him happier. This was how he pictured being a father, with sons and cricket. And he did it well. Other boys would come and without fuss he'd organise a pick-up game and it would go on till dusk and he would make a point of not favouring his own, indeed of doing the opposite. I think I understood, even then, that this was both deliberate and virtuous. Of course within a year or two even his youngest son didn't want to be seen with him. But if he felt betrayed he never showed it.

Adastra Park was two parks – the rougher lower one with the stream at its end and the more cared-for upper one where Terry the park keeper waged an endless war against dog shit and boys on bikes. At one end were the War Memorial Gardens whose dank shelters were a popular trysting place in summer for visiting French schoolboys and the plump local girls.

Two huge oak trees overarched a set of swings, the main pleasure of which was competition. Dave Collier was the champion jumper-off. This was done from a seated position. The aim was distance. The nub was choosing the moment to jump. It was an early exercise in practical physics. Go too soon and you hit the ground like a spinning wheel. Too late, like a sack of carrots.

The height competition was conducted standing up, your feet on the wooden seat, your hands gripping the iron chains. There was a point where you approached the horizontal and the energy of the swing faltered and the chains momentarily lost their centripetal stiffness. And in that fraction of a second just before you swung back down again you experienced an exquisite deliquescence of the bowel that I can sense even now, just I can smell the rust of the chain on my hands after swinging, like brown blood.

Further entertainment was provided by the jittery local paedophile. The story went that he was a former teacher, driven from the classroom by the creative cruelty of his pupils, who spiked his blackboard rubber with match-heads and booby-trapped his desk lid. He seemed a wreck. He stammered, trembled and smiled too much, and while he clearly didn't mind watching us run and romp and wrestle, he equally clearly was no threat. But that didn't stop older boys from leaping out on him and growling like beasts so that he'd squeal with horror and run away on tiptoe, gibbering as he went.

But above all the Adastra was the cricket ground I lived next door to. In April men started to appear on weekday evenings to prepare the square for the coming season. There was a temperamental reel mower in Wimbledon green that threw a fine plumed arch of clippings into the front catcher if you could only get it going. It left the square striped like a circus tent. To mark the boundary there was a four-wheeled miniature coffin full of sloshing whitewash, with a wheel at the back and another within the whitewash. To mark the line a third wheel, milled to a silky smoothness, was dropped in between these two to transfer the wash from one to the other and thence to the grass. The neatness of the arrangement never ceased to please me.

A cricket pitch is twenty-two yards long, a tenth of a furlong, a chain. And we measured out the pitch with an actual chain, a thing of metal links, each about nine inches long, that folded into a heavy and gratifying handful that belonged to the nineteenth century. We marked the creases with a brush and whitewash and a folding wooden frame like an easel. Everything about pitch preparation pleased me: watering, mowing, rolling, painting, filling and seeding the bowlers' foot holes.

Tom Docker drove the motorised roller. He was the big man of Hassocks cricket. Six foot something, bristle-haired, squeaky-voiced and built like a shire horse, he was our village Botham. As a bowler he trundled a few yards to the crease and then whirred his arms like some medieval siege engine. If his first ball of the innings was straight it would generally take a wicket, the batsman departing baffled, as if he'd been strafed out of a clear sky. As a batsman Dock had three shots: a block, a soaring heave over mid-wicket that threatened windows in Orchard Lane, and a drive through extra cover that curved like a scimitar, left scorch marks on the grass and once crippled a Dalmatian. Once, when fetching a ball from the War Memorial Gardens, Dock emerged dragging a trouserless youth. 'This little Frog,' he boomed, holding the rapidly detumescing offender up for inspection, 'was shagging one of our girls.'

Dock was single, effectively wed to the cricket club in summer and the working men's club in winter, where he played snooker. But every autumn when the cricket season had ended he would fly to Zakopane in Poland for a three-week tryst with a woman whom none of us had ever seen but about whom speculation was naturally intense. Dock also professed himself a communist. This manifested itself mainly in his being a union delegate at the engineering company where he worked, and also in his baiting of Cameron Symms with a 'y'.

Cameron was a genial young man who wore a cravat and drove a blue MG and had attended private school. There he had received the sort of professional cricket coaching that would have ruined Dock's game. It had made of Cameron an impeccably correct batsman whose every shot could have been an illustration from the MCC coaching manual except for the matter of hitting the ball. Dock's ridicule of him was one part athletic disdain, to three parts class warfare.

Also of a higher social class but never the victim of Dock's mockery was Barry Maine, a lawyer and ironist known universally to team mates and small boys alike as Fatty. The source of the nickname was Whitbread Tankard.

This was the late 1960s, when traditional breweries were being bought up in large numbers by the huge conglomerates. Real ale had not yet been identified as such so no one was out to save it. And in a world of thin sweet mass-produced beers delivered under pressure from metal kegs, Whitbread Tankard was down there with the worst of them. But Fatty drank nothing else. He drank it in camelish quantities and it seemed not to affect his demeanour. Ten pints to the good he would maintain the same ironic, self-deprecating inscrutability.

Every Saturday and Sunday in the season he'd arrive at the ground having lunched at the bar of the Langham Hotel. If we were batting he would take a deckchair to the far side of the ground and sleep it off. If fielding, he would station himself on the boundary close to the pavilion. When the ball was hit straight to him he would trap it under his foot and underarm it back. If it went more than a few yards to either side of him he would just let it by. But then, after a dozen or so overs, Dock would summon him to bowl.

Fatty bowled slow left arm around his belly. His run-up was precisely three paces and he claimed never to have spun a ball in his life. He saw bowling as an exercise in psychology. If the opposition were twenty for seven he would still place fielders on the boundary and expect them to get catches. If a batsman hit him for six Fatty would applaud. If the batsman got out Fatty would commiserate. He took a hundred wickets a season.

At Jevington I had been an infant and had seen the players as remote and godlike. At Hassocks over ten or more years I graduated from watcher to player, and I got to know them as flawed and interesting men. I joined them in the unlovely pavilion as they took off their weekend clothes and hung them on hooks around the walls and changed into whites. As they did so they exposed their astonishing bodies. Such variety. Such flawed flesh.

Dock's chest was a huge jutting buttress dotted with little outcrops of curly hair. Cameron's skin was white as milk, his breasts like a teenage girl's. Fatty's belly was a wonder, a perfect hemisphere tacked onto a gracile frame. And such underwear. This was a time when Marks and Spencer dominated the market, selling goods made only in the UK. I can see before me now Dock's vast and sagging knickers whose flanks were a sort of string lattice connecting a front and back of whole cloth stained by age and secretions. I stood and gawped in wonder at the freak show, at this parade of imperfection and variety, like Cortez and his men staring at the Pacific, silent in a dressing shed in Hassocks.

From the age of eight or so I wanted only to play cricket. Saturday and Sunday I'd turn up ready to fill in for a missing man on either side. If none were missing I did the scoring. Scorers are the unnamed chroniclers of cricket.

Most teams brought an adult scorer. Few were talkative. Many were introverted, made shy by some sort of flaw, a stammer, perhaps, or an orthopaedic shoe. Cricket has always attracted such people. And they made an art of their role. A cricket scorebook is a complicated thing. These people would make it more complicated still with a different coloured pen for each bowler, so that as the game progressed a thing of beauty would take shape on the page, like a pointillist canvas, until, when stumps were drawn at 7 pm, a game between, say, Keymer and Hassocks Second XI and Burgess Hill would have been turned for all posterity into an illuminated manuscript. And over the course of a season page was piled on page, every Saturday and Sunday the same, till by the end of September there was a *Book of Kells* recording in exquisite detail cricket that didn't matter. Where are those scorebooks now?

It was while scoring I witnessed my first death. The man was running up to bowl from the Memorial Gardens end when his knees buckled as if he'd been shot. He tried to run on, crumpled and fell. Everyone ran to him. Our house was closest to the ground and people ran there to ring the ambulance and came back with my mother carrying towels and bowls. The ambulance came in the wrong end of Orchard Lane and no one could find the key to unlock a gate to let it through. Players milled around. My mother passed me carrying a bowl of vomit with a tea towel from home over the top of it. Eventually the ambulance got through and was driven onto the ground, which was an excitement in itself, and the man was stretchered away and afternoon tea was taken and the game called off and we learned later that he had died in hospital. He was thirty-something. He'd had a stroke. I have cudgelled my brain but his name has gone.

Chapter 10

He was in his forties, I'd guess, a round-faced man with wet, fleshy lips and dirty teeth. He was a good club cricketer, a qualified cricket coach and an insatiable molester of boys. And the bastard gets a chapter to himself.

I was picked for Brighton Boys at the age of eight. It was the proudest triumph of my life to date. But he was there. In front of my father he grabbed me and placed me against his legs and tickled me to make me squirm and then he picked me up and held me upside down. He was laughing, and my father was laughing, but I knew immediately and irrefutably that he had turned me over in order to look down my shorts. I didn't know what to make of that knowledge. It would have been hard to find a more innocent eight-year-old. But I also knew that my father had no notion of what he was up to.

Over the next five years or so he was the snake in my Eden. Nothing could put me off cricket, or diminish my fantasy of becoming a professional player. But at every local level he was there to poison it.

He wasn't specifically after me. Indeed I'm sure I got off lightly. He was voracious in his appetites and not discriminating. I bet there are some out there who have far more reason to shudder at the memory of him. I further suspect that, like me, they will have felt powerless to act against him and too appalled to say anything.

Aged ten or so I was invited to attend winter nets at the county ground at Hove. To play cricket indoors in winter with proper coaching was an extraordinary boon, the clearest evidence yet for the existence of a benevolent god. I could barely contain my excitement. But he was among the coaches.

His self-indulgence was flagrant. As we boys changed into whites he would position himself for the best view of any exposed flesh, moving around the room as the viewing opportunities changed. When coaching a batsman who from fear moved away to the leg side, he would stand outside the net and poke a stump through it, its tip resting against the offender's backside. He would have argued, with some justice, it was a legitimate way of discouraging the retreat to leg. But it wasn't why he did it.

It was after batting that I dreaded. I would go back to the changing room to take off pads and glove and box.

If I was alone he would follow down the gap between the nets to join me. As I bent to undo the straps of my pads he would put his hands in my trouser pockets and fondle whatever he could reach. At the same time he would press his hardening dick against the crack of my backside and rub up and down through the cloth. All the while he would be talking about my batting, about the need for me to lead with the head when cover driving or whatever. I'd be quivering tense, my muscles rigid. I tried to concentrate on his words – he was a knowledgeable coach – and blot out the wordless violation, the hated contact, the despoiling. Pads off, I'd straighten up, he'd withdraw his hands from my pockets and step away and that was that. Nothing much really, and it never went any further than that. But it was a poison on my mind, a stain. I can still taste the misery it caused me both in expectation each weekend, and in retrospect on a Sunday evening. But I said nothing, did nothing, wrote nothing down, told no one and kept going to nets.

Is most predation like that? I suspect so. It was as though I were complicit.

I especially couldn't tell my father. If I'd done so, his response would have been forthright and fearless. But I felt as though this blight, this poison, belonged to a different realm of existence to the one he inhabited. It's as though I was protecting him from the sordid reality, he who was over fifty years old by then and who had fought in a war. His world and this bastard's had no point of overlap.

The end came simply. Sean Spart was a big lad from the bastard's own club. He bowled frighteningly quick and indeed went on to play a little first-class cricket. 'Is he bothering you?' he said one day, as we were queueing to bowl in the nets. Why then I've no idea. I nodded.

'Okay,' he said.

After I'd batted that day the bastard came into the changing room and did what he always did. Then Steve appeared. He pushed him off, sent him stumbling against the wall. 'Fuck off,' said Steve. 'Just fuck off.'

And he did.

Chapter 11

Cricket bewitched me. Football didn't. I played in goal because I was chubby, and better with my hands than my feet. Keeping goal also had the potential for Horatio-on-the-bridge heroism which very much suited me. I would pray for the opposition to bear down on goal so that I could make a save. If they scored I managed not to feel guilty. It was only football.

Our primary school pitch sloped so fiercely that a half-time lead of six goals was often overturned. For the downhill half I'd be a redundant spectator. For the uphill half, under siege. And it was during one such siege that a shot was heading for a corner of the goal and I dived and tipped it around the post and the crowd of maybe half a dozen classmates set up a chant. 'Jooo-lian, Joooo-lian,' they chanted, in imitation of a proper crowd at a proper stadium, and I had to turn away to grin.

One year the Mid-Sussex Primary School cross-country championships were held at our school. Quite why I was put in the school team I don't know. I was too plump to run well and I suffered from the stitch. The course started at the back of the school, then ran down alongside the football pitch past the goalposts of triumph, and over a stile to where a stream led through a little copse and out into pasture. Before us stood the scarp slope of the South Downs, a hump of pure chalk on the far side of which lay Brighton and the sea.

I was in the middle of the pack when the stitch struck. I heard other kids talk of running off a stitch. My stitch was unoffrunnable. It was a stiletto to the liver. I had no choice but to stop and gasp. The rest of the field streamed past, but for one. The kid in last place wasn't running at all. He was cheerfully and deliberately walking.

He was from Warninglid, a tiny village school. His entire year group had been made to take part and he was walking in protest. I walked with him. He was a revelation. Long-fingered, fine-boned, already at the age of ten he had something of the aesthete about him, something of the dandy. He didn't fear what the authorities might say or do. He seemed to be enjoying the walk.

We could see the others far ahead, now turning back up the hill towards the school and the finish line. And for the first time in my life I wasn't trying. I was good at school, good at sports, accustomed to praise, eager to win, obedient. And here was a taste of anarchy, of disobedience, of insurrection and it was ravishingly sweet on the tongue. Until, that is, we came over the rise and we could see the finish line and the already diminishing cluster of parents and teachers, my father among them. Duty flooded back across every synapse and I ran. I was no rebel. I was a good boy. Next to last was at least better than last. I didn't look back. I doubt the other lad was surprised or upset. He would have been already familiar with cowardice and betrayal.

When I crossed the line I was crying, and my tears were genuine, but they were not from pain. I fell to the ground clutching my side. My father asked what was wrong and I pointed at random at a kid from some other school and said he'd hit me in the stomach. My father went across to speak to the boy I'd fingered. When he came back he said nothing. He drove me home in silence. I bet the kid from Warninglid has lived a brave life.

It's odd how shame stays with you. My childhood has largely written white, but the shames remain in indelible ink and underlined. Like my treatment of Dean Cozier.

It began with a poem. I was walking Rebel along Dale Avenue in the dark. Dale Avenue was usually okay because of the street lights, but a fog came down. From one street light you couldn't see the next. You had to trust it would be there. I'd let Rebel off the lead and he'd disappeared. I called him and the sound of my voice in the fog alarmed me further. And I became frightened. Not cacking-the-pants frightened, but telling-myself-to-calm-down frightened. As a conscious prophylactic against worse I forced myself to compose a poem in my head. It began, and I am not making this up:

What, oh what is fear?
Is it not an aspect of the mind?

You may consider this a poor start to a poem but I promise you it gets worse. I bet it's the only poem in the history of English to include the phrase 'implement of human development'.

Nevertheless the act of making the poem stopped the fear from feasting on itself and got me home with bowel unbreached. Next morning the words I'd put together still seemed good to me so I wrote them down and showed them to Mr Tucker, who was our teacher and a nice enough man, I think. But he was no judge of poetry because he submitted my piece to some local journal of children's writing. And they were no judges of poetry either because they published it. Perhaps you saw it. It remains the only poem I have ever had published. I was horribly proud.

Then Dean Cozier wrote a poem. He was my chief rival for academic honours at school. He was more industrious than I but shy to the point of being furtive. When he worked he bent his head low over the desk and curled his free arm around his exercise book as a dog on a cold night wraps its tail.

Dean was more scientific than literary but the poem he wrote earned ten out of ten and a star from Mr Tucker. It was vaguely similar in rhythm and tone to my masterpiece. I accused him of plagiarism. I baited him. I abused him. I hissed at him. I reduced him to tears.

At worst he was guilty of imitation. My poem had been praised. He'd had to write one. It made sense to do something similar. And I probably suspected that this was how it had been. But I did not relent. He was muscling in on my success, climbing into my limelight, and I would not have it. Sitting next to him in class I so berated him that he curled up entirely on the desktop, his arms around his head and only his spine and the back of his head exposed. I kept going even at those until I saw that spine heaving and heard him whimper. I felt no pleasure. But neither did I feel pity.

Things got no easier for Dean Cozier. He reached puberty cruelly early. When the rest of us were pink and squealing shrimps, he had a bird's nest between his legs. At secondary school when we began to wisp up in crotch and armpit he was already shaving his shoulders. What cravings must have seethed and festered in his head while his classmates dreamed of pug and conkers?

The answer came in a divinity class when we were thirteen or so. The divinity teacher – how can such a title be bestowed or claimed? – was Mr Leppard, imaginatively nicknamed Spotty. He was an ambiguous character at best. His penchant was for leaning over you at your desk, and, while ostensibly taking an interest in your work, transferring everything in your right-hand jacket pocket into your left-hand jacket pocket without you knowing. It was Spotty who swooped down on Dean Cozier with the suddenness of an osprey on a trout and plucked from between the pages of the Bible a small format magazine – presumably small format so it could be read exactly as Dean Cozier was reading it – called *Forum*. It published letters ostensibly from male readers telling stories of improbable sexual gratification: 'I was driving to Aberdeen when two blonde Swedish girls appeared beside the road hitchhiking ...'

With a whoop and a ha, Spotty snatched the magazine and held it aloft. That cracking sound we all heard was Dean Cozier's psyche. He was not at school the next day nor the day after that.

Chapter 12

The eleven-plus was the first exam of our lives, a straight IQ test that acted like the swinging gate in the stockyard. If you passed you were destined for grammar school and an academic curriculum. If you were among the 75 per cent or so deemed to have failed you went to the ominously euphemistic secondary modern.

Brian Winters was the cleverest boy in the school. At the age of ten he spoke with the picky precision of the autodidact. I can hear him now reading his description of a car crash in which the victim's abdomen was crushed against the steering wheel. I greatly admired the word abdomen. I guessed it meant dick.

Brian Winters failed the eleven-plus. Perhaps he panicked. Perhaps he overthought it, saw traps where none were, presumed easy questions were actually hard. I was amazed to hear he'd failed, but far too selfish to care. Come the following September, I caught the 8.07 train into Brighton wearing the uniform of Brighton Hove and Sussex Grammar School, while Brian Winters took himself off to Hassocks Secondary Modern where my mother taught. It was two years before the authorities rectified the mistake.

The eleven-plus and the selective grammar schools were a product of a post-war effort at a meritocracy. They offered a quarter of the population an education modelled loosely on the private schools attended by the upper classes. We got Latin (but not Greek). We were divided into houses, though the use of the word was metaphorical. There was a school song and a Latin motto. Some of the masters wore gowns. And there was even a tuck shop, which was run by senior boys with limitless corruption. And it was an exclusively male world. The only women were the headmaster's secretary and the dinner ladies.

The first day was lived in terror. Second-year boys, we were told, would be roaming the school in search of new boys to hold upside down in a lavatory – the famous bogwash. When released from the classroom we gathered in groups in corners, like nervous herbivores. Nothing happened. By day two we were braver. By week two we were at home. Seven years lay unthinkably ahead. I told

Dave Collier that if we were both still at the school in seven years' time I'd give him £5. It was a sum of money as unimaginably large as seven years were unimaginably long.

The prefects were men, not boys. They had sideburns and shoulders. It was impossible to believe that we would ever be thus. (And of course, seven years later, when we were thus, we still didn't believe it. Some of us might be shaving but we sensed that manhood had somehow shrunk.)

Teaching ranged from the incompetent to the inspired. Bill Bone taught French and promised a free period every two weeks if we were good. In reality free periods came about twice a year but that only made them the more memorable. Bill used them to tell stories. He was a Cockney in his sixties and he didn't think it beneath him to amuse small boys. I laughed so hard during his story of being a guide on a mountain train in Switzerland that I was in pain.

More importantly, Bill opened the bonnet on language and showed me how it worked. After two years with him I'd grasped the whole grammatical structure of French. After that there was only vocabulary and idiom to learn. And it was through French that I learned how English worked as well. I'd probably have got there without him, but it was Bill who gave the ball a shove that has rolled throughout my life.

His antithesis was the art master, known to one and all as Killer. We heard of him before ever we got to school. Rather than deigning to make little boys laugh, he made them dread. Kids forged sick notes to avoid him. He conducted fingernail inspection carrying a sword. When we did italic lettering he would stand behind us with a huge stapler. The moment he saw an elbow lifted from the desk he would leap on the culprit with a banshee scream and staple his jacket to the desk.

Once you reached the senior school he became affable, presumably because he knew his antics would be seen through. But by then the damage was done. In later years I saw art teachers who actually taught art, who brought good stuff even out of kids like me who had no talent. Killer induced only a desire to ditch art at the first opportunity.

Between these extremes, the teaching was traditional and competent. Chalk boards, textbooks, surnames, homework, end-of-term tests, end-of-year exams, constant rankings against each other, and promotion or demotion according to performance. It suited me. I was keen and worked hard and did well and wanted to top the class and sometimes did and never once, not once, was I called a swat or a creep or a teacher's pet, which still strikes me as remarkable. I was innocent, heart-whole and happy.

The headmaster was a skinny man whose most memorable quality was his lack of memorability. Tellingly I can no longer remember his actual name but he was unerringly christened Weasel. It captured precisely his lack of presence, his slyness and his habit of sniffing the air. He presided without enthusiasm over the weekly assembly, which consisted of a token hymn and an even more token muttering of the Lord's Prayer, whereupon the doors in the side of the hall opened to admit a couple of dozen Jews and Catholics. Quite what risk to their religious beliefs they would have run by attending assembly I can't imagine.

The Jews and Catholics were supposed to file across the hall and stand as aliens in plain view of the seated rest of us. Understandably they balked at that and despite the urgings of the prefects they clung to the walls by the door where they'd come in. As far as I am aware they were never subject to any form of discrimination. No one cared about Catholics because no one considered themselves Protestant. Or indeed Christian. And though there were obligatory jokes about Jewish meanness, the Jew of the joke was not the Jew of the classroom. Many of the Jewish kids were among the most popular.

In sum, then, the secondary education I got was secular, academic, fair and entirely free, and I was blessed to get it. Even the train fare to and from Brighton was paid by the local authorities.

In 1968 Hassocks railway station was still Victorian. It had a ticket hall, a waiting room with a coal fire, a waiting room for ladies only, a gabled roof, ornate ironwork, a stationer's shop, a stationmaster and a staff in uniform, each with a whistle and a sense of status. By 1975, when I left school, Britain had gone through the three-day week and rolling power cuts and vast inflation and loans from the IMF and the station had been demolished and everything mentioned in the list above had gone except for the stationmaster's whistle, and in their stead had arisen a new spare, mean station with no shelter and no amenities that just cried out to be graffitied and was. Instantly. But none of it, naturally, impinged on us at the time.

Brighton was twelve minutes in one direction, London an hour in the other. On the opposite platform every morning was another of the warnings that Hassocks gave its children: the mass of commuters bound for the capital, many still brollied and bowler-hatted and even stiff-collared. They stood in the same groups in the same places each morning and carried the same newspapers, mainly the *Daily Telegraph*. The warning was not lost on me. In English I wrote story after story about commuters imprisoned first by an office job and a routine and later by a lunatic asylum.

The journey to Brighton included Clayton Tunnel, which had 113 joints in the track, each creating the familiar clackety-clack of train travel. For first-years it was an unending source of joy to mentally tally them and then at 103 to start counting down out loud from ten. On the count of one the train would magically burst back into daylight. So engrained did this habit become that I would count the 113 even without consciously choosing to do so. More remarkably still, when they laid continuous track and thereby did away with the clackety-clacks, I could still hear their ghosts, count them down and predict the moment of emergence to within a second or two.

A sticker above every window on every train bore the legend 'Do not lean out of the window'. We all knew of the schoolboy who leant out just as a train came the other way, and of the other schoolboy who leant out just as the train entered Clayton Tunnel. Both reeled back into the train headless. And of course we all still leant out of the window, partly because the possibility of decapitation lent glamour to the act, and partly because the pressure of air on the roots of your hair was elemental – and what boy does not rejoice in elemental? – but mainly because many of the trains had handles only on the outside so you had no choice but to lean out of the window to open them. As the train drew in to a platform the doors would open along its length like leaves unfurling from a stem, with a boy at each door judging the moment when it was possible to jump. Time it right and you got the minor honour of being first. Time it wrong and you were going faster than you could run, with the result that you were flung rolling along the asphalt. The head-to-toe abrasions hurt less than the humiliation.

The adult commuters to Brighton were fewer and less formally dressed than those heading to London, but they were still sufficient in both number and formality to make travelling to school with Dave Collier a perilous exercise. Dave had mischief in the way I had obedience. He was free of malice but he loved to test all limits. If seated next to a commuter with a newspaper Dave would make no secret of reading it. Then when the commuter went to turn the page he'd indicate with a gesture of the hand that he hadn't quite finished yet. More often than not it would work.

He would initiate games that defied etiquette, that challenged good manners, that were subtly seditious of good order. When they became too funny to resist I'd find the courage to join in, would wind them up a notch, would invoke a reaction, would look to Dave for approval and find he'd gone. I came to dread assembly on Wednesday mornings. 'Those pupils who were on the 8.21 from Hassocks to Brighton will stay behind.' Dave and I would be required to hunt down the adult who'd complained and apologise. Being in trouble made me feel unwell. Dave only found it funny. Why he stuck with me throughout our schooldays I don't know. Maybe conformity and cowardice appealed to him as nonchalant irreverence did to me.

Chapter 13

I had no particular aptitude for maths or science but no difficulty learning the stuff. And I found some pleasure in the logical patterns of arithmetic and algebra, and was happy enough in Dim Jim's class working through a column of quadratic equations of increasing complexity as the afternoon sun moved across the pale cream walls of the classroom and the brown-cased clock ticked steadily towards the end of school.

But after doing maths O level in the fourth form we came to additional maths in the fifth and a fork in the road. Add maths was taught by Nobby Clarke, a dapper man who favoured sharp suits and hair cream rather than the tweedy fustian worn by most masters. Nobby had a son with inch-thick glasses who arrived in the fifth form and immediately founded a Conservative Society and was therefore, and quite rightly, persecuted. But it wasn't Nobby Clarke's fault that I struggled.

Add maths involved calculus. I did not understand calculus. I would learn by rote the formula for, say, differentiating a quotient – and could repeat it now, half a century later – but I did not know what a quotient was, or what it meant to differentiate it or why anyone should want to. But others did. I could see them seeing how calculus applied to reality and asking questions I could not follow. It was a watershed moment. Here was a fundamental difference between the nature of my mind and the nature of others' minds. The gulf between the hard science of higher mathematics and the softer science of grammar and linguistic patterns is an actual gulf. And it was in Nobby Clarke's class that I learned on which side of it I stood. For my A levels I fled to languages.

I'd done two years of Russian. This was the early 1970s and while the British Empire had effectively dissolved, the Soviet Union appeared only to have grown stronger. So the school offered Russian presumably out of geopolitical pragmatism, taught by Toby Turl, an affable man as bald as a billiard ball, who didn't, as it happened, speak Russian at all well. But I loved it. It had the romance of the exotic. I relished the grammatical complexity and the new sounds I had to tame my tongue to, and the unfamiliar flourishes of the thirty-three letters of the

Cyrillic alphabet. To this day I write my capitals Ds as Dostoevsky would have done. But the school didn't offer Russian at A level.

So I did A level Latin. I was the only taker for it. It was taught by J. B. Williams, a bluff and hearty man, and a dedicated pipe smoker. He was also the librarian, so our daily class took place in his little office, which had no ceiling. While I parsed Livy or Virgil, the office would become so full of smoke that I had to lean in to see the text and the smoke would billow up and over the sides of the office as if from some chemical retort and boys pretending to study in the library would pretend to suffer from coughing fits. J. B. never seemed to notice.

What I liked about Latin was the grammatical architecture – ablative absolutes, pluperfect subjunctives, the cascading sequence of tenses – and the untranslatable concision of, say, the 'et' in 'timeo Danaos et dona ferente'. But classical literature didn't sing to me, didn't chime with the life I was living, didn't do what literature exists to do, which is to give a jolt of recognition, a sense of yes that's how it is. I got that from my other two A levels.

In French we read Camus. 'Aujourd'hui, maman est morte. Ou peut-être hier, je ne sais pas.' That sang. That went straight in. It was the first book that mattered to me.

I stole Sammy Barnes's copy – I'll come to Sammy by and by – and have it still on the shelves beside me as I write. Above his signature on the flyleaf in thin black ballpoint are the school stamp and the words 'Issued To' and below it, 'He is responsible for keeping this book in good order.' I've kept it in good order for forty-seven years.

The other book stolen from school and on the same shelf is Larkin's *Whitsun Weddings* and that was Jack Smithies' fault. My English teachers till then had been forgettable. Everything I learned about the language I'd got by proxy from French and Latin. And I'd been given nothing to read that seized me, that gratified me. At home I read little but cricket books. Then in the sixth form I had Jack.

Jack didn't so much teach as simply be Jack. There was no gulf between the teacher and the man. And he was funny. Not making-children-laugh funny, not rehearsed-joke funny, but alive-to-irony funny. He found the world a comic place and we were welcome along for the ride if we fancied it. I fancied it. His was an adult mind I could plug into.

I'd have found my way to literature regardless, I suspect, but it was Jack who introduced me to Austen, Pope and the all-shaking thunder of *King Lear*, and it was Jack who tapped me on the shoulder in the corridor one day and suggested I might like Philip Larkin. I signed *Whitsun Weddings* out of the school library that afternoon. On the train home I read 'Days' and 'Ambulances'. That evening I read most of the rest of the thirty or so poems, turning the thick pages with greed. The following morning I signed the book back into the library, crossing out my name on the card to prove that I had done so. Then after school I went back and stole it.

It didn't feel like theft. Larkin's words were my inchoate thoughts and feelings made verbal crystal. He wrote of an imperfect world where 'nothing's made as new or washed quite clean', and he did so with such clarity, such honesty and such simple beauty of utterance. He wrote of the dissatisfaction, of the dread that 'lies just under all we do', of the brooding presence of death and futility. This was what could be done with words and it was a thing very much worth doing.

I take the book down now. The cloth boards are held together by a sort of worn gauze on the spine. The school library card is still in its pocket at the back with my name crossed out. I taught hundreds of kids from its pages. Introduced them to Mr Bleaney, to the sadness of home, to life being 'slow dying'. And, as Larkin observed, saying so to some meant nothing. Others, it left nothing to be said.

I can remember no one thing that Jack Smithies taught me, no ideas or insight or wisdom. What mattered was how he was. Here was one who on reaching man's estate had not fossilised, had not assumed a guise. Funny is what I keep coming back to. Jack was awake to the strutting folly of the human condition.

Some thirty years later in a London pub, Michael Simkins, the actor, whom I was meeting for the first time since we'd been at school, told me Jack Smithies was dying. He gave me his phone number. I hesitated. I owed Jack plenty but to acknowledge that debt only when he was dying seemed like an afterthought at best, a conscience salver. But I rang.

'Mr Smithies, Jack,' I said. 'This is Julian Bennett. You may not remember me but ...'

'Remember you!' he said. 'I've still got the scars.'

It wasn't true. But it was a great line. His voice, though, was thin and raspy, like the dried hair on a coconut shell.

'I'm going to be in Brighton,' I said. 'May I come and see you?'

'I'll never forgive you if you don't,' he said.

His flat was on the fourth floor of an undistinguished block near Preston Park. When I got out of the lift he was waiting on the landing, hunched and tiny in a dressing gown and slippers. Cancer had eaten him to a husk. There were tufts of grey hair on his cheeks and his cheekbones pushed up sharply beneath them. He shuffled back into his flat and dropped into a soft chair and fell asleep. I thought of leaving. But he woke within a minute and spent the next half-hour making me laugh.

Teaching had been his life. He'd toyed with writing, had had a couple of small things published when he was younger, but it seemed too precarious a living and so he'd taught. He'd stayed at the one school for his whole career. He'd never married.

In recent years many of his past colleagues had died. A former pupil ran the local crematorium and whenever he caught sight of Jack arriving for another funeral he'd emerge from his office, seize Jack by the arm and ask in a Dickensian whisper, ''Oo is it this time, Jack?'

Though he was now weak as a kitten, and all but dead, he was still Jack. I could sense exactly what had drawn me to this man when I was in my teens, and he still enjoyed making me laugh. There's a performance element to teaching. We didn't speak of his imminent death, at least not explicitly. I guess he was in his early seventies. His sister was tending to his few needs. His wasn't a life that needed much wrapping up.

When I left I shook his hand of bone and skin. I told him not to get up. Across the other side of the road was a small park. It was a windy day. Kids were playing football with sweaters put down as goalposts. I turned to look back up at his flat and he was standing in the window. I waved and he waved back.

He died a couple of weeks later. His sister attended the funeral, along with several hundred former pupils.

Chapter 14

When I was eight, Dave Parsons, who had laughably prominent knees, explained the facts of life to me by drawing diagrams with a stick in the mud of the Adastra streambed. Which was more than my father ever did. As far as I could tell, my parents were sexless. They occupied separate beds. I never saw them do anything but peck a kiss of hallo or goodbye, no hugs or fondling or hint of physical intimacy. I found the word love embarrassing.

At secondary school I duly stared at the occasional copy of *Mayfair* but my aim was to discover the precise anatomical lie of the land and for this the pornography of the day was of little use. But the jokes got raunchier and one by one my classmates revealed in the showers increasing quantities of armpit and pubic hair while I remained smooth and pink and acorn-tasselled. I remember sitting in the changing room at the county ground at Hove where I was playing for Sussex Under Fifteens. Across the room sat Simon Heffernan naked, announcing that he was picking 'last night's come' from his bush of black pubic hair. I wanted to go up and study it. I was theoretically aware of semen but only in the vaguest sense and was probably still a year away from production. But there were stirrings.

Aged fourteen or so I was walking past the Hassocks Hotel to which our affable retired next-door neighbour Bill McGill drove at noon every day in his white Triumph Dolomite, and back from which he drove some two hours later with magisterial slowness. But now out of the front door of the hotel came a youth in a pair of purple hipsters, which were, as the name suggests, trousers that sat low on the hip.

He was seventeen or so, a trim compact figure, with long hair down his back, but it was his hipsters I stared at and followed and was pleased by. And at that moment I was somehow aware, without guilt or distress, that this was the side of the fence I stood on. It didn't feel sexual, though I didn't know how sexual felt. It felt aesthetic. I found his body pleasing to look at, no, more than pleasing – beautiful, gratifying. The youth walked up the steps to the railway station and then turned down into the underpass, which was white tiled and smelt of piss. I watched him go, then caught the train to Brighton to go fishing.

And that was that. My ideal form was male not female. And I think I had always known it. Poof was the word we used then. A poof was a recognised type, distinctive in speech and manner. I had classmates who were already distinguishable as poofs. But I didn't see myself as one of them. I just preferred my own kind.

Puberty arrived at five in the morning in the form of the only wet dream of my life. I cannot remember the subject of the dream. I cannot forget the astonishment. No one had told me to expect anything like this. Here was a chemical brain bath that outdid every pleasurable sensation by a factor of ten. No wonder the world sang to its tune. When the experience proved to be repeatable within a few minutes, the world had changed.

Three decades later I met an electrician brought up in in the East End of London whose most poignant memory of coming of age was his father shouting up the stairs, 'Will you leave it alone for *one* night?' That was not the sort of family I belonged to. When I put my pyjama trousers out to be washed you could have snapped them. My mother never said a word.

My fantasies were indistinct. Girls featured because somehow that was expected – the power of conformity can reach even into the imagination – but as climax approached they became secondary or androgynous figures and the central figure would be an attractive youth. As his rainbow burst so did mine.

It was all intensely private, not to be raised with even my closest friends, most of whom were making increasingly dramatic forays into the world of straight sex. Bob Moore was rumoured to have spent the night in a dormitory at Roedean, the poshest of private girls' schools, perched high on a cliff to the east of Brighton, a beckoning challenge to the red-blooded. And puberty stirred some of even the least obtrusive into action. Martin Smith had always had the knack of self-effacement. He rarely spoke, never came first or last, was okay at all things, but notable at none, could be absent from class with few people remarking on it, but when puberty called he answered with a view halloo so resonant that he became, by all reports, the most dedicated besieger of maidenheads in the south of England.

I did not. I tagged along once or twice to discos where the noise made my head ache and the girls sniggered at my dancing. I made an occasional self-conscious effort to engage the sort of girl I could almost fancy myself fancying – narrow-hipped, flat-chested, short-haired – but none reciprocated and I soon gave up.

The only fellowship of sexual feeling I sought or found was in books. I was acutely awake to the homoerotic, and suspected that I alone saw it. The short stories of Saki were especially fertile ground – his lithe youths, his baby-snatching Pans, his defiance of starch and order in the form of maiden aunts and deep repression sang to me. I held it all to myself like a poker hand.

Meanwhile the associated qualities of adolescence kicked in. I went from bright enthusiast to disaffected sulk. I grunted to adults, neglected schoolwork, grew my hair and all the dismal rest of it. I continued to play cricket – some loves run deep – but I had recognised by now that I would never make a living from the game.

I'd been doing odd jobs for a while, delivering papers, marking papers up for others to deliver, cleaning out the fridges in a fish shop on Saturday mornings, picking fruit and vegetables in season, and on my sixteenth birthday I blew all I'd saved on a moped, a Mobylette from France, light blue, underpowered and unreliable. Unlike my brothers I had no mechanical nous or interest in vehicles. But this bike, with its 49cc engine and the pedals that helped it uphill, was a passport to everywhere, a snapper of apron strings, a simple assertion of self. I rode it sober and I rode it drunk and I wrote poems as I rode it, wrote them in my head and recited them to the rushing wind and once in a while I crashed the thing but was never going fast enough to do myself or the bike much damage.

And I rode it once to Newhaven to fish and that was the other conger eel I promised you. The breakwater that guarded the harbour was a long curved mole of concrete that took the brunt of the Channel's weather. There was a colonnade that ran the length of it on the seaward side under which you could shelter when fishing, leaving your rod propped against the harbour wall, fishing into the comparative calm. In good storms the waves thudded into the structure with a force you could feel with your flesh and sent huge plumes of spray over the colonnade to land with a sizzling thud on the concrete and to drain away through holes in the wall. A good place to be.

On this particular winter's day a fat man in a donkey jacket hooked a conger and the usual crowd gathered and the beast was hauled up with the help of a drop net. Once on the breakwater it somehow sloughed the hook and writhed on the concrete. It was maybe six feet long and as thick as a thigh at the front end and it was the colour of the winter sea, all mottled grey and brown. Men jumped back from it as it writhed, except for the fat man, who was trying to kick it to death with his heavy boots but was not making any progress until another man stepped in and stood on the beast's neck and a youth emerged from the crowd to stand on its thrashing tail. The youth wore dirty white plimsolls and he was beautiful. I can see him now, half a century on, this Adonis, this Antinous, this Ganymede. I can see his jeans, his ribbed sweater, his pale hair, but there is no point to the catalogue. The point was the sum of him. The point was a beauty I could not take my eyes from.

While he was helping to subdue the fish I could legitimately, if not stare at him, at least look his way. When the fish was dead, its killers, the youth included, stepped back in a ring of reverence around the corpse, while Fatso, smiling, posed with rod in hand in the manner of big-game hunters everywhere, as if the death of the beast conferred some virtue onto him. Then everyone drifted back to his own rod, leaving the conger inert and bloodied on the concrete, much shrunk in size.

I followed the youth because I had no choice. When he stopped at his rod I carried on past, then turned again to drink him in. And so it went on that afternoon. I moved my gear near his. I feigned motives to walk past him – to kick seaweed back into the water, to watch a man land a small pout whiting.

What did I want? To be noticed? To say hello? I doubt it. I'd have jumped if he'd spoken. And it would have diminished him. For I had idealised him on sight, adopting by instinct the ancient fallacy that beauty and character are tied. But all that is analysis after the fact. What I felt at the time, and more strongly than I had felt any other feeling, was the gravitational pull of beauty, an approximation of the ideal form. It was not long after this that I first read *Death in Venice*. I understood it immediately.

When the youth packed up fishing for the day, so did I, and I rode home on my moped with a freight of self-knowledge.

Chapter 15

And then my father died. It was the cigarettes. He'd smoked all his life and everywhere he went. Most men did. I never minded. Indeed, I liked the smell, and by now had started smoking myself, though secretly, away from home. His brand was Guards, a white packet with a red stripe and a picture of a guardsman in a bearskin.

It happened quickly. He began to get headaches. He went to a hospital in London for tests and was there for a while. When he came back he seemed weakened. He must have known he had cancer and was seriously ill, but neither he nor my mother told me and I didn't mind. By then I was the last one left at home and I have no doubt they were protecting me.

One evening I returned from school and there was a note in the kitchen on what to cook for my tea and then my mother rang and said that my father was back in hospital and she might be late home. I ate and watched television and I think I knew what to expect and so I didn't go to bed and some time after midnight my mother came home and she'd been crying and I'd never seen that before.

And she opened her arms and hugged me and wept on my shoulder and I registered for the first time that I was taller than she was. 'Your father died tonight,' she said, and I looked over her shoulder at the framed reproduction map of Sussex and the grey telephone on the hall table and my first feeling was of relief. I thought of the things that I could now get away with. For with a little motorbike and booze and smokes and hair to my shoulders and the attraction to all things dark that comes with adolescence I already knew that I was butting up against my father, just as my eldest brother had done. But unlike my eldest brother I had no stomach for the fight.

My mother had been driving my father to the hospital for an appointment that afternoon when he had haemorrhaged in the car, to catastrophic effect. She flagged down a truck driver who drove off to call an ambulance, leaving my mother to tend to her husband as he bled to death in the passenger seat of a Fiat 500. And while my mother told me all this I thought only of myself.

The next morning I had a Latin exam, and as I rode my moped down the A23 I found that, if I thought of my father, tears came, tears that the wind drove back from the corners of my eyes, but I felt no grief.

My mother must have called the school. At the end of the exam the deputy head met me at the door of the hall. I told him I was fine, found my bike, drove away up Dyke Road and then turned around and went back to school. I pretended to myself that I needed to fetch some books, but I was going back to boast, to milk the moment. I wanted others to know that I knew death, that I'd seen the big thing close up, that I was tinged with it. I knew it was a shitty thing to do but I did it all the same.

I chose to look subdued. By the notice boards I saw Martin Harvey, a kid I had little to do with, and asked how he was doing and how he'd found the exam, and then he asked if I was all right and I said, 'My father died last night.' (I had mentally rehearsed the line and chosen after some internal debate to say father rather than dad.)

'Oh,' he said, 'oh, I see. I'm sorry.' And I felt awkward for him and was glad when he made an excuse and left, and I left too and drove away on my bike, aware that I'd failed to exploit the occasion and ashamed that I'd tried to. Do we always remember moments of self-revelation? I don't know. But this one's seared in the skull.

Years later I came across a poem by Edward Lucie Smith in which the young narrator is taken aside by the headmaster of his boarding school and told that his father has died. The boy is duly upset but something else stirs within, and later when he enters assembly and all his peers fall silent and look away, 'pride, like a goldfish, flashed a sudden fin'.

My father had been fifty-eight. My mother was fifty. In just a few years three of her four children had left home, her husband had died and her main income had disappeared. It would have been nice if her one remaining resident son had climbed above his adolescent self-absorption and offered her a little love, a little support, or had just recognised that she was having a hard time. But he did no such thing.

When my mother died at the age of ninety-seven my brother found among her things two letters from my father, marked, in her hand, 'First and last'. The first was written in 1944, shortly before D-Day, when my father was stationed in Eastbourne where my mother had been raised. She, by then, was at college in Croydon.

My Dear Joy
Great soldiers tell us that battles and life are basically pretty well the same; to win the former

one must have speed and surprise, so I presume that to be successful in the latter it's necessary to have speed and surprise. Anyway, I've only got ten minutes to spare just now so I'll have to be speedy, and I'm probably going to surprise you; with these two elements, according to the formula, I should be successful. I hope so.

Do you think you could arrange to come home this weekend? So shortly after your holiday it does seem a lot to ask, but my reasons for asking are extremely sound. Time doesn't allow me to quote them, otherwise I would, but I will stress that I wouldn't miss the chance of exploring your 'haunts' without first making every possible effort to achieve it.

So if you can come at such short notice, either send me a wire or phone 2787 when you arrive and we'll explore, even if it rains.

Your letter did me a power of good. I'll give you the answer later.

Here's hoping.

Sincerely yours

Gordon

They married in early 1945. The last letter was written from the London hospital in 1973.

Darling Joy

I've just had a visit from a cheerful intelligent nursing sister to tell me that all the lovely food I ordered for Friday has been cancelled. I am due in the theatre at 10.30 am. I shall try and ring you myself in the evening.

Nurse has encouraged me to wander around the third floor for exercise and to talk to people. There appears to be no shortage of staff here, no sign of crisis anywhere.

Mr Brown has just been to see me – just a chat and to confirm the 10.30 appointment.

Thanks to you, darling, your love, care (and cooking), I don't think I could have come here in better shape. I am not feeling low or afraid – my basic feeling is a determination to return as soon as possible to look after you and share with you so many of the things we are going to do together.

All my love, darling

Gordon

Chapter 16

It was love, of course. His name was Sammy Barnes. He'd been an unobtrusive classmate for five years, winning no prizes, quiet, mildly subversive, given to a curl of the lip at absurdity or pretension, a sneer even. The crowd he ran with, if he ran with any crowd, were the less keen, the more rebellious, the somewhat disaffected. *If* was the film. The Stones were still the music.

He was pale and skinny and his ears stuck out. But overnight and simultaneously, like seeds responding to a shift in the temperature of the soil, we had all grown our hair long. And puberty took the blandness from our faces and rearranged our features a bit. Some coarsened, grew blue-chinned. Sammy became beautiful.

Until then the world and I had been in synchrony. What it wanted for me I wanted for me as well. But now, well, it was different. There began a period of intense introspection, self-delusion, self-pity, self-dramatisation, selfishness. And no other period of my life has been more vivid or more formative.

The week centred on Friday and Saturday nights in Brighton. Brighton was a good place to be adolescent. It had a track record from Graham Greene to Mods and Rockers and the bank holiday fights that set the country in a moral panic. In summer it was a down-market resort that had already lost out to the Costa del Sol. The piers were no longer a novelty, the weather was English and the beach stony. In winter the tourist shops shut and the displays of Brighton rock and sugared icing, moulded and coloured to look like bacon and eggs or a pack of puppies, collected dust. The rain beat on the windows and the sea crashed on the beach. Winter in Brighton had a seedy quality that suited the adolescent mind. And there was an abundance of pubs that were only too happy to serve underage drinkers.

The Posada in Ship Street was where things began on a Friday or Saturday night. As the name suggests it was an effort at a themed bar that had failed and simply sunk back down to being a pub. But to me it was a place of myth and wonder.

There might be gentle Paul who thought for himself and could draw, hunched Nick who had a Trotsky quality and a tolerant mum, Sid who had a rich streak of gloom, strange dogmatic Steve, stammering Willy who had a sweet independence or fierce Rob who scared me with his fearlessness and threat of anarchy. But it all hinged on Sammy. If he was there the evening had a lustre. If he wasn't, it was dead time, time without point or hope.

What he made of me I don't like to think. I must have fawned after him like a puppy. I yearned to give him presents, fought the yearning because I knew it gave me away, yet still succumbed to it. I gave him *Death in Venice* with an added epigraph that I cannot now recall. But I can recall mulling over whether or not to write it, knowing it would be disastrous to write it, and then writing it. 'Oh thanks,' he said when I gave him the book in the Posada, and he put it in his jacket pocket unopened. *Death in Venice* wasn't right. Aschenbach was too old and Tadzio too young, but it was the best I had. Male beauty, infatuation, unfulfillable yearning and death.

I wanted Sammy to myself. I wanted to own his beauty, though not his flesh. I had only the vaguest notions of gay sex and none of it appealed. The Sammy I loved was Sammy clothed. I wanted him in jeans and T-shirt and battered second-hand jacket. I wanted him as he was in the Old Steine late one night. Sid was driving the overloaded Hillman Imp and I was following on my little motorbike and up ahead there was some sort of police road block and we all stopped. It was a damp winter's night, late, and the wet road glittered as if star-strewn. And Sammy went on ahead on foot to see what was up and I watched from behind as he stepped up the sparkling black street amid a dazzle of car lights and street lights and flashing police lights and he was just a slim but haughty silhouette in jeans and old suit jacket, the collar turned up, and a cascade of hair, and I ached for him. When I think of him now that's the image I see, urban, wintry, adversarial.

I was rich with despair and more than half in love with easeful death. Sammy had a long fur coat, got like most of our clothes from one of the dim little shops on North Road that were crammed with the wardrobes of the dead. I fantasised about Sammy finding me dying and cradling me in his arms against the fur of that coat. Every bit as much as wanting him I wanted to be him. I tried to dress like him and there was no surer way to intensify despair. The sort of jeans he looked faultless in wouldn't pull up over my thighs. Collarless shirts on him looked the essence of proletarian chic. If I wore one I looked like what I was, a middle-class creep trying too hard.

I wasn't the only one to whom Sammy mattered. I sensed that others were attracted not so much to his beauty as to his apparent self-assurance. I saw every one of them as rivals. And the same was true of Sammy's girlfriends. They were several and all quiet, faunlike and lovely.

Josh Patten had a sister of whom boys spoke with hushed reverence. It was Sammy who turned up with her in the Posada one evening. The same happened with another fabled younger sister, within a few hours, it seemed, of her having turned sixteen. Both girls had the pallid slim innocence of early Renaissance Madonnas, the child-brides of fourteenth-century Florence. The thought of Sammy bedding them filled me with an exciting yet sickening ambiguity.

One Friday after the pub shut, I gave Sammy a lift home on the back of my bike. We kept to the backroads because I was drunk and he had no helmet. It was a summer's night, balmy, and we were lightly dressed. He put his hands on my waist as I drove and Brighton held a radiance. Sammy lived near the school. I drove past his house onto the school playing fields.

I was still living a double life and was due to play cricket there the next day. I drove the bike up and down the cricket squares and then to the end of the field where an assault course of ropes was slung among trees. We clambered about on the ropes for a bit and swung down

116

with the ease of drunks. I stopped by the first eleven pitch on the way back and dismounted to do it damage. The ground was hard and rolled and dry and I had only my hands, but it was an offering to Sammy. Clawing at the ground till my nails broke and bled, I pulled away enough of the pitch surface on a good length to render it, if not unplayable, at least dangerous. The priest was desecrating the altar.

The next day I arrived late at the ground having arranged to meet Sammy first for a lunchtime beer at the Good Companions on Dyke Road. He didn't show. I expected the match to have been called off because of the pitch, but play was under way. We'd won the toss and were batting. I went in at four and there was nothing wrong with the pitch. On the next pitch over, however, I found the damage wrought by my scrabbling fingernails, too insignificant in sunlight for anyone to have even noticed. A rabbit scrape of defiance. As if the night before had barely been. I batted with a breezy carelessness and got seventy. My pleasure at the runs felt like a betrayal.

My night-time self was drawn to the idea of seediness but I was only playing at it, a dabbler lured by the low lights. I liked the drinking. I especially liked the smoking and spent hours on technique: the inward striking of a match, the cupping of the hands around the cigarette, the precise but nonchalant tapping of ash into the tray with a pecking forefinger, the blowing of smoke rings. Cigarettes were adulthood in a box. To have twenty Carlton and a box of matches in your jacket pocket was to feel equipped.

But I was no anti-establishment rebel, no counter-culturalist, and I wasn't interested in drugs. For sure I sat in late-night bedrooms and passed around the sodden roll-up in which allegedly there burned a sprinkle of hashish acquired in some covert deal in the pub toilet. But I never bought any myself and most of the stuff others bought had no more effect on me than the sawdust it may well have been. I did once take LSD, but I rapidly tired of the brightly coloured imagery. I had enough going on in my skull already. There were also proper drugs about, especially heroin, but the few glimpses I got of that world scared me.

A youth called Eddy Foster used to hang around with us, despite being two years older and having long since left school. He liked to play the role of underworld roué but the truth was he had no friends of his own age. I hated everything about him. He was disreputable, seedy, unclean. He made me squirm with distaste. I was my father's son far more than I cared to admit.

In the Heart and Hand one Saturday night, two men came through the corner door, seized Eddy by the collar, dragged him off his barstool and across the floor and out the door screaming. By the time we got outside they were kicking him down the alley between the pub and the Greyhound next door. They were kicking for keeps, sinking the boot into his foetal form, into his ribs, his crotch, the arms folded around his head. I just stood and watched. Others, including Sammy, tried to intercede but these were big and violent men.

When they finished with Eddy and turned away he abused them from the ground and they turned and came back at him again with the boots and left him bleeding and whimpering. We helped him into the Greyhound, sat him in a corner out of sight of the landlord. It had been something to do with drugs and a motorbike. I didn't want to know. Others took him to hospital. His jaw and forearm were broken and he'd lost teeth. I felt no sympathy, only revulsion at the violence and a desire to stay out of whatever world that came from.

Chapter 17

It was an unimpressive time. I brooded on suicide. I was just conscious that it would be a cruel blow to my mother, but that's as far as any degree of selflessness or thoughtfulness went. I was as egocentric as a toddler and moody as thunder.

In Nick's kitchen late one evening I sawed across my wrist with a serrated vegetable knife. It hurt, but it bled only superficially. Even if I'd known to go along the vein rather than across it I still doubt I'd have managed it. Sammy came into the kitchen. 'What the fuck are you doing?' he said. I mumbled something, rejoined the others and then offered Sammy a lift back to his place. By now the Mobylette had died and I'd graduated to a slightly larger Honda. On the side of my crash helmet I'd painted, badly, a dripping bullet hole. With Sammy on the back I drove through the early morning streets, ignoring stop signs, driving blind through junctions, giving fate a chance if it wanted it. As far as I could tell from his hands on my waist, Sammy didn't flinch.

It was a race between growing up and screwing up. Screwing up won. One weekend I acquired the keys to a cricket club bar. After the pubs shut I led everyone there, me on the bike, everyone else in Sid's Imp. Sid was Eeyore, famously and unaffectedly lugubrious, with a sense of imminent doom. But he never missed a party and drove the Imp everywhere, spectacularly crammed with writhing seventeen-year-olds whose hair spilled down their backs.

We were drunk when we reached the club, drunker when we left. (I put some money in the till on the way out: not enough to pay for what we'd drunk, but enough to feel less larcenous.) The Imp had a flat tyre and no spare. I offered to drive to an all-night garage. Sammy climbed on the back with the tyre. The garage we found in Patcham had no interest in mending a puncture for teenage drunks at one in the morning. At some traffic lights on the way back Sammy tapped me on the shoulder. The unmarked car behind us had policemen in it.

In a bid to get away up the A23 I crashed the bike into a grassy bank. Both Sammy and I were thrown off but uninjured. I was breathalysed and arrested, the bike confiscated. The arresting officer was called Constable

Hooker. They took Sammy's details then let him go, but drove me to the Brighton police station and held me in a cell until a doctor could be roused to take a blood sample.

At 3 am I was given the choice of leaving then or sleeping the night. I left then. It was a warm summer night. I walked the dozen or so miles back to Hassocks, going over the South Downs via Ditchling Beacon as the sun rose. Larks sang. Black-faced sheep grazed the springy turf. The weald of Sussex was laid out like a green checked cloth and the air was as fresh as tomorrow. It was a lesson in the indifference of the beautiful.

My mother was getting up when I got home. I told her I'd been arrested and went to bed. She just sighed.

Sammy and I went to court a couple of months later. An officer read out the endorsements already on Sammy's driving licence, even though he'd never owned a vehicle. The year before he'd filched his father's car then written it off near Devil's Dyke. On the advice of a lawyer at the cricket club I'd had my hair cut and wore a jacket and tie. The magistrate was the standard-issue old booby: gin-reddened, bespectacled, sententious, a suburban Polonius. He warmed to me and loathed Sammy. He urged me to turn towards the light, banned me from driving and levied a fine of £200, which was, to the penny, what my grandmother left me in her will that same month. She'd have been appalled. So would her son.

When I look back, that was the apex. The wave had peaked. Thereafter came only the long slow subsidence, but it's lasted a lifetime. That period of my life remains a background hiss to everything, like radiation from the Big Bang.

I'd screwed up the mock A level exams. That shook me. I did enough work to make sure I passed the real things. The school wanted me to sit entrance exams for Oxford or Cambridge, which would have meant staying on an extra term, but I was eager to leave. I meant to take a year off and go to Australia. I had a notion of working my way down through France and just keeping going, south and east. Beyond Italy my geography grew hazy. Beyond Constantinople it stopped as abruptly as for a seventh-century monk. But from there it could only be a few further hops. And Australia had allure for me still. It was partly because of memories of lying in bed on frozen nights in February listening to John Arlott's commentary from a sunlit Sydney Cricket Ground. But it was also because it was as far away from home and family, and effectively myself, as it was possible to go.

Straight out of school I signed on for the dole. This was England in the mid-1970s under Harold Wilson. The queue at the Brighton dole office was long and the hall it trudged through might have been designed to depress. It took an hour to reach a guichet where a bored official sat behind thick steel mesh. I got £12 for that week, felt ashamed and guilty and soiled, and never went back. I worked at odd jobs all summer – building sites, pubs, a discount bookshop – saving up for the journey I told myself I would begin in the autumn, and perhaps never return from. Though I was daunted just by the thought of it.

At the end of the summer half a dozen of us rented a motor boat on the Thames for a week before we scattered. From that trip I have my only photograph of Sammy. He is looking quizzically into the camera, leaning on a hatch, his old black sweater worn through at the elbow, his mane of hair unkempt, his chin and upper lip dusted with yielding youthful stubble. I have the photo before me now on my desk and to stare at that face is to sense the backwash of feelings that are close to half a century old. If my house caught fire today, it's this photo that I'd run into the flames to save.

At an approach to a lock gate Sammy mistimed his jump onto the mooring, slipped and fell backwards into the shallow water, his limbs spread-eagled, his hair fanned out like Ophelia's and his eyes wide in disbelief. I laughed as he fell, then reached down to haul him out.

One night we were the last two back from the pub and Sammy went down into the boat among the sleeping and emerged with a bottle of Sandeman ruby port and we climbed a tree with it, climbed higher than I would have dared to go alone or sober, and we sat up there overlooking the river that shone like new steel, and we passed the bottle between us. I had Carlton cigarettes, the packet a royal purple, and I passed one to Sammy and he cupped his hands around the flame of my lighter and the image of his face lit from below had a beauty that made me gasp.

We stayed up there an hour and finished the bottle then swung down through the branches and crept aboard the boat full of muttering, breathing sleepers. Sammy slept in a sort of alcove near the door of the cabin. Later that night I clambered out past him to piss and it was a warm night with a full moon and in sleep Sammy had thrown open his sleeping bag and lay there, ivory white and skinny in a pair of battered dark-blue Y-fronts.

And that was pretty well that. In the forty-five years since, I've barely seen him. When at university he spent a year in France and I wrote to him there. To my surprise he wrote back, using squared French notepaper. The tone of the letter was friendly. He mentioned Erich Fromm's

To Have or to Be? – Sammy had always had an idealistic streak. And perhaps that text had something to do with the last line of the letter, the envoi: 'Know what you are and be it, creep.'

Perhaps four years later I came back to the UK from working overseas and in a pub in Brighton I bumped into Sammy's father. He told me with an exasperation that he didn't try to hide that Sammy was living in a squat in Camberwell. He gave me the address: 'Try and talk some sense into him, will you.'

I put off going to Camberwell for a couple of months, found excuses for my own fear. I had images of squalor, of Sammy ruined and raddled on bare floorboards, ravaged by drugs and poverty like Sebastian Flyte in Algiers, and me an awkward bourgeois intruder. But at the end of the summer, my last day before flying off abroad again, I went. It was hot. The building was an old tenement block of yellowish London brick. A youth with freckled milk-white shoulders and a Union Jack singlet was lounging on the steps, smoking.

'He's in the nick,' he said. 'Brixton.'

It seemed that Sammy had been working overseas and before he returned to the UK he had posted himself a block of hashish. When he went to collect it at the post office the authorities were waiting for him.

126

I was a Tube ride from Brixton but I found reasons not to go. At Heathrow the next day I bought *Rebel Angels* by Robertson Davies and sent it to Sammy c/o the prison. I hadn't read it. The title was the point. Eighteen months later the book came back to me stamped 'Unknown at this Address'. I read it then and didn't think much of it.

Some fifteen years later I dedicated a book of my own to Sammy. It was only right to tell him. By now the internet made it easy to find him, especially as I knew his date of birth. He was born on Christmas Day. I had a phone number for him in five minutes. I shook as I dialled it. I recognised his voice immediately, the lazy sub-Cockney of Brighton, allied with a world-weariness that he'd always had and a sense of irony, as if disappointment was the norm, but with a grim comedy to be drawn from it. We talked together as middle-aged men but I still felt like a supplicant.

A while later, Sammy sent me an email. I've kept it of course. Here's how it ended:

So are you coming to England? I would like to see you.

I enjoyed our phone conversation. There is room here to kip the night – in fact you are welcome to stay a while if you are in need of a base.

That northern summer I went. We met in a pub by the Ouse.

Beauty is rare and ephemeral. Few have it. Fewer still keep it long. It means nothing, but it makes things happen, it moves people. Beauty's had more effect on my life than any other external influence. Sammy's had gone, of course. His hair had thinned, his skin coarsened. But I could see the ghost of beauty in the arrangement of his features. And he remained lean and upright, a handsome man.

He had a daughter, aged nine, who lived with her mother just up the road. The following day we took her around Lewes Castle, where we read plaques about Simon de Montfort, and Sammy held her hand as she walked along the top of walls, and I bought us all ice cream.

Sammy lived in a rented flat under the roof beams of a building however many centuries old that looked out over Lewes High Street. Life had not been easy. A prison record hadn't helped, though it had been an open prison – whatever that might mean – rather than Brixton. He'd settled to no career, no profession, but had kept up with technology and had just secured a poorly paid job with some internet outfit. He was vegetarian.

When he went off to work the next morning, leaving me in possession of his flat, I leant for a while at the sink by the little casement window, my elbows on a chopping board where Sammy had buttered toast, and I looked down over the old High Street of Lewes and thought about Sammy. I saw him in double form, as the middle-aged man thwarted by bad luck, and as the youth in whom I'd seen, rightly or wrongly, everything I wanted in this world: beauty, courage, insouciance and quiet but firm rebellion.

He was to blame for none of it. I doubt we'll meet again. He mattered more to me than anyone.

Chapter 18

I went to rugby training at Haywards Heath, was tackled, heard a snap as I fell. The coach came running, said, 'I hope that wasn't what it sounded like.' It was, and nastily so, cleanly across the tibia just below the knee. I was in plaster for three months.

Jack Smithies rang and said that since I couldn't be going anywhere I might as well sit Oxbridge entrance. No need to come back into school, he said. I should just read. So I lay on my bed and smoked and read. And after three months I could blow a smoke ring as thick as rope that hung quivering on the still air of the bedroom for twenty seconds before disintegrating. I read most of Hardy, weeping at *The Mayor of Casterbridge*, and all of Larkin – though all wasn't enough, and Dylan Thomas (though there was nothing to compare with *Under Milk Wood* that we'd read with Jack), and Austen, Trollope. Maugham, Saki, a few of the more recondite Shakespeares – *Titus*,

Timon – in order to drop their names, and the whole of the *Albatross Book of Verse*, which began with 'Sumer is icumen in' and ended with 'Only one ship is seeking us'.

With all this newly ingested I swung into school on crutches to sit the entrance papers, and wrote a series of essays that I'd like to read again now because, however callow they may have been, I meant them as I wrote them and they came with a rare fluency and urgency; they came like rivers.

I went to Cambridge for an interview in the new year. I'd applied to Queens' College because I'd stayed there once during a cricket festival and had been given a room under the eaves with a little dormer window, as in that improbable painting of the death of Chatterton, and late one night I'd climbed out of it and up onto the roof with Geoff Cocksworth, who was a sweet and gentle guy with a mass of curly hair, and we'd sat astride the roof-ridge for an hour or so that warm and starry night and looked out across the roofs to King's Chapel, the expanses of lawn and the mist rising off the river.

The only other interviewee I met was a blue-chinned Jewish lad, cocksure, expensively educated, infinitely better read than I, who let me know within a few minutes that he'd once been dandled on E. M. Forster's knee. I'd not heard of E. M. Forster and I'd been dandled on nobody's knee; indeed the first person I met who'd written a book was the man who interviewed us both, a medievalist who'd edited the bits of Chaucer I'd been unimpressed by at school. He was a precise and nervous man in slip-on shoes and though he was scrupulously courteous we did not get on. I'd praised Shelley in my entrance papers. He described Shelley as an adolescent taste. I knew he was right, and indeed had already seen through Shelley, but I maintained my position, as one does. I did not expect to get in.

I was in bed at home a month later when my mother brought up the letter with the college crest on it. She had been unable to wait for me to get up. I hadn't realised she felt so strongly. I opened the letter, read the few lines. 'I got in,' I said, flatly, though I was pleased.

My mother was overjoyed. She kissed me. I feigned indifference, damping her delight. I knew it was cruel even then. She'd been adopted, brought up poor, had her youth stolen by a war, had struggled to become a teacher, had given up even that while she raised a family and here was a reward by proxy, and I stamped on it. I gave nothing. I barred the emotional door. That must have stung. It is hard to forgive. But it was some odd compulsion to keep my feelings private, to close things off from my family. I feel it still. I don't know why.

My leg was mended, my future settled. I had six months before the clock restarted and if I was going to go to Australia I had better start soon. So I did, half-heartedly, quarter-heartedly, packing an army surplus rucksack and setting off without saying where I was heading because I knew I wouldn't get there, but I had to go through with the charade so I could tell myself that I had tried. I left Hassocks on foot and stuck out my thumb to get to Newhaven and the cross-channel ferry. I got as far as Lewes when darkness came. I had little money – I was going to pick fruit in the south of France – and I spent a grim night in a bus shelter, knees to chest on the narrow bench, head on the coarse canvas of the rucksack, eyes open most of the night from fear. In the morning I caught the bus of ignominy home.

And instead of picking grapes in the south of France I got a job as groundsman and cricket coach at a prep school in Birmingham. It was my introduction to the parallel world of private education and how far parents will go to keep their children from mixing with their social inferiors. In doing so they threw them into the care of some of the oddest people I had ever met.

The headmaster was a fat and fervent Christian who treated his wife as a domestic drudge. If he wanted coffee he would flick his fingers. If he spilt his coffee he would wordlessly beckon her to clean it up. And his greatest pleasure was preaching biblical morality to nine-year-olds who sat cross-legged on the floor and looked up at him with beaming incomprehension. His second greatest pleasure was cricket.

Like a lot of cricket devotees he was hopeless at it. In the annual staff against school cricket match he faced one ball, missed it, was called to run a bye, somehow got his pads entangled, tripped and fell and was lying on his back mid-pitch when he was run out. I had to turn away to laugh. The boys didn't bother to turn away. He sulked for the rest of the day.

The women on staff seemed quiet and competent. The men didn't. The old boy who taught French was a former military man with a close-cropped white moustache that told you most of what there was to know about him. He did not like little boys and they reciprocated.

The humanities were taught by a pudgy middle-aged man with a goatee beard who lived in the school as a tutor in the boarding house. He had a penchant for the higher arts, a penchant he broadcast by playing Verdi or whatever at high volume with his window open. Proclaiming it his mission to educate the philistine cricket coach, he persuaded me to go with him to the opera at the city hall. He'd chosen a comic opera, he said, to ease me in. I found it about as comic as herpes, but still slightly more comic than sensing my companion's arm casually draping behind my seat during the second act and the hand coming to rest with a butterfly lightness on my shoulder. Hardened a little by experience, I brushed it off. No reference was ever made to it and neither was the mission to educate the philistine continued.

But it was hard to imagine a better job. I was in charge of the cricket field. It was the famously hot summer of 1976, in which cars spontaneously combusted and cricket matches were cancelled because of the ravines that opened up in the parched land. But not on my field, which remained the colour of a Dorset water meadow all summer.

The school was deep in the suburbs. A hundred houses overlooked the playing field. Fully half the householders must have emerged over the summer to complain about my watering regime. I sent them, as I'd been instructed, to the head, and what he said to them I don't know, but none came back.

My days were spent on the gang mower and the roller. I weeded every last daisy and plantain from the square by hand. I marked out the pitch for a house game as if it were the Lord's test. My hands grew callused. My skin darkened. And I coached the under-nine-and-a-half eleven to an unbeaten season.

My star player was James Nutbrown. He was a scamp in constant trouble. The old boy who taught French detested him, but to me he was another Mike Mitchell, the kid with the charm and the courage. His mother came to a match one weekend. She was barely thirty, long-legged, oozing a knowing sexuality. 'James,' she said, 'has told me *all* about you', and she laid such stress on the 'all' that it was halfway between an accusation and an invitation. 'He seems to have appointed you his new dad.' I was nineteen.

On Wednesday afternoons we played other prep schools in the area but never a state school. Many of the prep schools were old country houses tucked away up long drives on what had once been private estates. We'd be greeted on arrival by one of the resident staff, often a foppish young man of dubious tastes, himself a product of this parallel system of education. The staffroom, where we drank a pre-match thimble of sherry, was always the same, with a notice board, class lists, some battered books and old items of sports gear. Waugh's *Decline and Fall*, written fifty years before, was still bang on.

The fop and I would umpire the match and the fop would cheat on behalf of his boys. I cheated only once. James Nutbrown was run out on about forty. As the appeal went up he turned to me with wide and pleading eyes. 'Not out,' I said, and I saw him smirk. He went on to get fifty. No one scores fifty in the under-nine-and-a-halfs. It was mentioned in school assembly. Corruption starts small.

I was sometimes asked to cover in the classroom. I soon learned I had a talent for winding kids up, but none for winding them down. In an impromptu history lesson I was halfway through a re-enactment of the execution of Charles I, complete with James Nutbrown as hooded executioner, a prostrate Charles, his neck stretched over the wall-mounted pencil sharpener, and a crowd of twenty chanting 'Off with his head', when there was a knock at the door and a child with a folded note from the moustachioed old bastard who taught French in the room next door. The note was written with a fountain pen, in an italic script so tightly formal you could sense the clenching of his teeth. 'Would you care to control your class?' it said.

I despised the man but I was scared of him. 'Execution off,' I announced. 'Oh sir,' groaned Charles I, 'that's not fair', but he accepted the reprieve. Not so Executioner Nutbrown, who was leading the crowd in a resumption of the chant. 'Enough,' I said but James wasn't about to stop enjoying himself. He was beating time on a desk with his executioner's axe, a hockey stick.

Faced with the prospect of the bastard next door stepping into the classroom, silencing it with a glance and then addressing me with some pseudo-courtesy chosen with the sole purpose of further humiliating me in front of the kids, I grabbed James by the shirt front and pushed him harder than I'd meant to against the blackboard. The ledge that ran along the blackboard's base as a repository for chalk and board rubbers, jammed into his back. He screamed. The silence was immediate.

'James, I'm sorry,' I said, 'are you all right?' but the damage was done. He had tears in his eyes and he flung down the hockey stick and stomped to his desk and buried his face in his arms on the desktop.

In the staffroom half an hour later the old boy sneered at me over the top of the *Telegraph* and I have rarely hated a man more.

But the job suited me. I liked tending to grass. I liked coaching cricket. I liked arousing a class of kids, getting them eager, seeing their faces light. I liked making them laugh. I liked the kids themselves. And I very much liked being liked by them. And thus began a long and fruitless struggle against teaching for a living. Since accepting that I'd never be a professional cricketer, I'd fantasised about writing, thought vaguely about journalism, even more vaguely about the law, but made only one decision, which was that never, under any circumstances, would I teach.

I was suited to teaching, for all the very reasons that I didn't want to admit. It flattered my vanity. It offered easy theatre, and a safe miniature world, a form of tiny kingship over the young and powerless. But however it might suit my nature, to me it smacked of cowardice. Instead of going out into the world and forging something new, to go back to school was to retreat from the unknown to the known, the obverse of adventure. To teach would be the external undeniable expression of my lack of courage.

And yet, I could already sense it threatening, as if my hull had just made contact with the faintest outer current of some distant whirlpool and though it seemed that I was sailing freely, my destiny was inescapable already, that I was slowly being drawn in.

On that last day of the summer term, with the kids packing up classrooms and parents picking up the boarders in their large cars, there was a knock at the door of my little triangular bedsitting room. 'I made this for you in pottery,' said James Nutbrown, and he handed me a chunky conker-coloured coffee mug. 'But it sort of collapsed in the kiln, sir.' The rim was bent like a sine-wave. He put out his hand to shake mine. When he left I cried. I used the mug for years.

Chapter 19

Sid, gloom-drenched as ever, gave me a lift to Cambridge. At the porters' lodge a plump, bespectacled boy with a führer fringe and a college scarf, like a prefect in a Bunter book, greeted what was presumably an old school friend. 'Giles!' he squealed in an accent that belonged in the same Bunter book. 'Oh Giles. How splendid.'

'Good luck,' said Sid. He was off to Reading. A fortnight later he sent me a postcard of Reading University Library. On the roof he'd drawn a stick figure leaping, labelled 'Me'. I've not heard from him since.

To me Giles's friend represented everything I feared Cambridge might be, a playground for public schoolboys, drenched in ritual and privilege. Over the next three years I never exchanged a word with him, but I saw him around the place and held him in my mind as a totemic warning. I remember his name without difficulty half a century later and if you'll excuse me for a moment I shall put the terrible power of the internet to work. Well, it seems he became a missionary.

I had never liked the name Julian. It smacked of the Famous Five. It was nice and white and middle class and earnest. It seemed to embody all the qualities I liked least about myself. If ever there was a time to change my name, it was now. Childhood was over. I was starting afresh in a new place with no one who knew me. I resolved to become Jack. The name was strong, simple and brave. But somehow, when it came to introducing myself, I couldn't do it. It felt deceitful. Then fate stepped in in the form of a bewitchingly beautiful medical student from Belfast, who shook my hand at some introductory function and said, 'You're Joe, aren't you?'

Mute with momentary adoration I nodded and became Joe. Oddly enough, it made no difference. Once a Julian.

I read English because I got a thrill from *King Lear* and Larkin, a thrill I didn't get from chemistry or maths, a thrill of recognition and of beauty and of truth. Literature crystallised in words what I had imprecisely sensed. I read to know that I was not alone. Also I hoped to write. But it became clear very soon that reading English had nothing much to do with any of that.

The first two years were a straight chronological bash through the highlights of the English literary tradition from *Gawain and the Green Knight* to *Women in Love*. I quite liked *Gawain and the Green Knight*. In the third year you specialised a bit.

Attendance at lectures was expected but not compulsory. I went to five in my first week. Two of them baffled me. The other three evinced none of the delight in literature that I had come for, and I knew, even then, that academic literary criticism wasn't for me. I didn't want to learn its rubrics, its jargon. I wasn't interested in literary scholarship or historical context. I belonged in the literary appreciation class. I sought only the buzz, the rush, the thrill.

So for the ensuing three years I went to no lectures at all, apart, that is, from a single lecture in physiology at the urging of my friend Dan. He wanted to show me a girl he considered the most beautiful in all creation. I found her unremarkable but the lecture a revelation. It was on equine diuretics. I still recall, handily, that if you inject a horse with a solution containing potassium ions the beast will fill a bucket within seconds.

So my weekly duties consisted of a single timetabled hour, my meeting with a supervisor at which I was expected to produce an essay and generally did. My first supervisor was the medievalist who'd interviewed me. He once treated me and another student to a reading of *Piers Plowman* in the accent and pronunciation of the fourteenth century – though how they knew how it was all pronounced I cannot tell you.

'In a somer seson,' he intoned, 'whan softe was the sonne', and as he did so he absentmindedly slid his socked foot out of a shoe under the desk. But the shoe was new and stiff and when he tried to slide the foot back in it didn't go. He continued to read, all the while reaching for the shoe with his foot and forcing it further away from him and sinking a little lower in his chair. Eventually the toe of the shoe peeped out like a shy little animal from under the far side of his desk.

The one person on the faculty at Queens' I would have liked to be supervised by was the resident professor, who had a reputation for abruptness. He was a minor poet and dressed the part, crossing the winter quad in a beret, an army surplus parka, a leather satchel at the hip with his strap slung across the chest like a bandolier, and holding hands with a middle-aged grey-haired woman. But though he stopped once to gaze at me, when I was working thirty feet up a ladder painting gutters, I never actually met the man. Indeed the Queens' English department gave up on me quite soon and quite rightly.

Thereafter I was farmed out for supervisions to an assortment of characters dotted about the university town who had little or no connection with the college.

The first of these, whose job it was to guide me through the Renaissance, was a graduate student little older than me. She had cheekbones you could have cut a steak with, and she sat cross-legged among cushions and joss sticks and chiffon wall hangings. She despised the poetry of Donne on the sole grounds, as far as I could tell, that he was a bloke.

I didn't last long with her or any of the others I was sent to, each seemingly further beyond the college walls than the one before, until finally I arrived at the eighteenth century and Valerie Grosvenor Myer. I stayed with her very happily for the remainder of my time.

Valerie lived fifteen miles away in Ely, and came to my rooms once a week. Sometimes I'd still be in bed and we'd talk through the wall and she made coffee while I had a piss in the bedroom wash basin and pulled on a pair of jeans. She was in her early forties, childless for reasons I didn't know, married to a teacher-cum-folk singer. She had been brought up poor in the Forest of Dean, left school at sixteen, but then went to night school, got into Cambridge as a mature student, earned a first in English, wrote books on Margaret Drabble and Jane Austen, and hung around the university, reviewing theatre, freelancing and sometimes jobbing as a supervisor for such students as me.

Somehow she never quite cracked the academic establishment, perhaps because she was a generalist, an old-fashioned lover of the written word with little time for critical theory. But it was for matters beyond literature that I relished her. She had a clever open adult mind and there was nothing she would not discuss. The least productive part of the supervision, which would often go on for two hours or more, was the discussion of literature.

One morning she arrived pale and shaken at my rooms and by way of explanation unfolded her lapel. Hidden on the back was a badge with the legend, 'Yes I'm homosexual too.' At the urging of a friend she had worn it openly on the bus into town. The abuse she'd received had shaken her. The year was 1977.

In two years of supervisions the only thing I can remember her teaching me was that the past tense of slay was slew and of slew slewed. But teaching is more than the things taught. Teaching is a transmission between people. Teaching is personal. Valerie was the first adult woman I ever got to know and I owe her a debt of thanks. She became a friend and we corresponded for the next thirty years.

In her seventies she was crippled by Parkinson's disease. When it got too much to bear she resolved, typically, to take her own life. If her husband were present when she died he might be considered legally complicit, so they agreed that he had to be away from the house. On the morning she chose to die they said their final goodbyes and then he went off to the university library for the day. She took her overdose but never made it to the bed where she meant to die. He returned that evening to find her splayed on the floor. The story became national news and was much quoted in the debate over assisted dying. She'd have been proud of that.

Of the cohort of ten or so reading English at Queens' only one lad was ever going to get a first-class degree. I saw him recently on television. He's inevitably a professor now, still quiet, precise and thoughtful and a world authority on a novelist little read outside university English courses. I do not envy him.

I thought it best to avoid a third-class degree if possible, which left only a second-class one. So, for three years I read the books I needed to and one night a week I locked the door of my room and filled the coffee pot and wrote an essay, and at the end of each year I did enough revision to squeak through the exams and into the year that followed.

Second-class degrees came in two varieties, 2.1 and 2.2. I had friends who sacrificed pleasures in their pursuit of a 2.1. They ate the charcoal biscuits of wakefulness;

they waxed their ears to the call of the bar. I thought them misguided and so it has proved. In the big world beyond the university walls, only one person has ever asked me what level of degree I got. A NatWest bank manager, from whom I was seeking an overdraft, took his pipe from his mouth, though it remained connected by a sagging rope of spittle, and said, 'So, Mr Bennett, you have a university degree?'

'Yes,' I said, 'a 2.2.'

'Tell me, Mr Bennett, is that better or worse than a first?'

Best of all, five years after I had graduated, and at the cost of, I believe, £5, the BA Cantab. metamorphosed into MA Cantab., as my reward for having skilfully carried on breathing. I could have declined such indefensible privilege, of course. It never crossed my mind to do so.

The upshot of all this was that I had abundant free time. Early on I took up boxing, mainly to convince myself I wasn't the coward I knew myself to be. We trained twice every weekday, running backwards in the dawn across Parker's Piece, throwing punches at imaginary opponents, and at the gym at Fenners in the afternoon throwing punches into a hanging bag or the padded fists of the coach. He was straight out of the 1950s with a white singlet and Brylcreemed hair and he called us all 'sir'. I hit him once in the stomach without meaning to and it gratifyingly doubled him over but somehow did not prejudice him against me.

Indeed I was the first of the new recruits to be given a bout. My opponent was Rupert, a public schoolboy in his third year who informed me quite early in the piece that he was related to Orde Wingate. The remarkable thing about that, it seems to me now, is that Rupert took it for granted I would know who Orde Wingate was.

I jabbed at Rupert's face, moving about the ring on my toes, keeping my guard up, and jabbing again, all as I'd been taught. I sensed that boxing was going to be the making of me. Then Rupert punched me on the nose. It stung. My eyes watered. He swung a right. Instinctively I turned away from it only to meet a left coming the other way. My skull rang between his fists like the little hammer on an old-style alarm clock. I wrapped my arms about my head. The blows kept coming. I turned my back. The coach stopped the fight. I left the ring and the gym and never went back.

I had more success rearing a thrush. I found it late one night as a nestling on the ground and I took it in and fed it warmed milk from the empty tube of a Bic pen, and later, as it gained size and plumage, worms. I called it Prendy after the vicar with doubts in *Decline and Fall*. The bird lived in my room in a cardboard box that I covered with a towel at night. During the day he had the run of the room, would greet me with a frantic rush of wings whenever I came in. If I sat at my desk to write, he'd perch on my hand and peck at the pen. I took to walking around the college with him on my shoulder, until a day when tourists stopped to photograph us and Prendy took fright.

But he came back, reappearing later that afternoon on top of the dormer window of my fourth-floor room. From the ground I called with the kissing noise I made when feeding him and he came fluttering down on the instant and landed at my feet and my little heart swelled. I took him out onto Queens' Green then, turned over some soil and for the first time he stabbed himself a worm, and I decided it was time for him to take his chances in the wild. I tossed him up in the air and he fluttered back down to my feet, and I tossed him again and he fluttered back down, and I tossed him a third time and he flew and perched in a tree overhanging the river and I went back to a room where every surface was redolent with bird shit.

But what mattered to me was finding friends. Prejudiced against anyone from a private education, I cultivated kids from grammar schools, pleasant young men with northern accents.

The most engaging was Dan from Lancashire who'd asked me to the lecture. He was a brooding natural scientist with black eyes, lithe flesh and a nose like a shark's fin. Before a rugby match he'd eat a bowl of boiled potatoes. He was brought up Catholic and his conversation hinted at depths of turbulence. I liked him best when drunk. Five pints to the good he'd shed the dowdy plumage of the young Lancastrian chemist and become the angel of misrule. Two or three nights a week we'd go out on the town and perhaps one of these would end with Dan clicking over into Mr Hyde.

He'd throw a glass, steal a bike, come running out of the dark to effect a textbook rugby tackle – shoulder to midriff, driving with the legs, wrapping the arms – against some innocent scholar returning late in the evening with a pile of books from the university library. I got a fearful thrill by association.

One evening I called at his room and he said he wasn't coming out. That wasn't unusual: he often needed convincing – there was guilt in there. But this time he persisted.

'All right,' he said as I continued to harry him, 'here's why, but you'll laugh.'

I said I wouldn't laugh.

'God held me down.'

'Oh, for fuck's sake.'

'God held me down in this chair, pinned my arms. I couldn't move. He gave me a choice. Either I could go drinking with you or I could choose him. Whichever I chose he'd let me go but I had to make the choice.'

'So it's me or God?'

Dan nodded. I laughed.

But Dan was unbudgeable, adamant, calm.

I went to the bar alone, got drunk, came back to Dan's room late, woke him, told him that he'd been indoctrinated, that if he'd been brought up godless like me he'd be godless, and so on. Dan heard me out and nothing changed.

I took a while to relent, to concede the defeat. Another night I burst in very drunk on a meeting of the Christian Union that Dan was holding in his room, a dozen bland young men sitting about with tea and cake and open Bibles. They were alarmed but Dan took me in hand and led me into the bedroom and I was sick in his wash basin and he put an arm around my shoulders as I heaved and the sink blocked and he reached in with his finger and swizzled the bigger bits down through the grating.

I missed Dan but he wasn't the one. Halfway through my first year I read *Brideshead Revisited*, and I recognised myself immediately in Charles Ryder. I, too, sought that low door in the wall that opened on a world of enchantment. I, too, sought a Sebastian, a Sammy, who would love me back. Unlike Charles Ryder, I didn't find him.

But I did fall in love again, more gently this time, more cheerfully, but no less one-sidedly. Inevitably it was with a public schoolboy.

The Kangaroos was a college club for athletic drunks. I was invited to join in my second year, as was a lean tall rower, with huge hands, a soft voice and a face reminiscent of the young Jagger. Tim was studying engineering. His friends were mainly fellow engineers and rowers, tall and confident young men from public schools, young men with rich accents and a frivolity that Sammy would have looked askance at. I would have, too, had it not been for Tim. He did not lead his group of friends but he was central to them in a way neither he nor they acknowledged or perhaps were even conscious of. People loved Tim. His appeal was innocence. He seemed unblemished, a child with a man's hands. And he was beautiful.

I started to seek him out, to inveigle my way into his life. It wasn't easy. He went to lectures in the morning, rowed in the afternoon, drank less than I did and had a girlfriend in a distant college. Moreover I didn't belong with his crowd. But I persevered and became a friend, a sort of pet alien in the group, state-school, non-rower, under six foot, a drinker, but mildly amusing.

I was jealous but careful not to show it. And there were good drunken escapades. Tim was another in the catalogue of climbers I have known, always likely to shin over a wall or up scaffolding onto a roof. But behind the carefree climber there was a darker self, a suggestion of some pit or wound that he touched only when very drunk. One night of group partying he locked himself in a toilet at the bottom of T Staircase and would not emerge. Everyone else moved on to more revelry but I stayed and sat on the wooden stairs, their treads smoothed and rounded, and talked to him through the door and tried to discern the source of his distress. I never did get to it, but that there was something there, some bulb of inchoate misery, only added to his allure.

I didn't mope for Tim or feel wretched. I laughed and drank with others and played cricket and rugby and squash, and was raucous in the college bar, but in my final year the measure of a good day was whether I had spent part of it with Tim. I would have loved to have been his only friend. That was the extent of my ambition. He smoked Rothmans so I did too. For the next thirty-five years of smoking I went back and back to them, could never see the blue and white and somehow magisterial packaging without a pang of remembered desire.

Of course I wondered about being queer. The word gay had only recently been appropriated and there was a small brave university Gay Soc that held an open meeting in a pub across the road from Queens'. I positioned myself at a corner to watch a few people go in, saw no Ganymedes among them and did not join them. It was largely fear, but also uninterest in what I understood to be gay sex. That just wasn't it at all.

I have dwelt on Sammy and Tim because I dwelt on them at the time. I have found it very hard to find the words to tell the truth of the time. Were they just adolescent crushes? Perhaps. But both mattered to me greatly, then and now.

Sammy and Tim were from opposite sides of the tracks. They had two things in common. One was beauty, the other fearless honesty. Both seemed only themselves, and I, who felt like a chameleon, found that captivating. One night in the Granta, overlooking the river, drinking pints of Abbot, Tim told me he didn't know how to lie. And later that same evening he told me I was going to be a teacher.

Chapter 20

'I expect you'll be becoming a schoolmaster, sir,' says the porter to Paul Pennyfeather, in *Decline and Fall*. 'That's what most of the gentlemen does, sir, that gets sent down for indecent behaviour.'

Waugh himself had taught for a couple of years, as had several of the writers I admired – Betjeman, Eliot, even Auden. For all of them it had been something they fell back on, an interlude, a stopgap measure. I didn't want it to be even that but I'd done nothing about finding something else to do. And I would have to do something. I was broke.

Money had played little explicit part in my childhood. It was as unmentioned as sex. My father was the standard breadwinner. I had no idea how much he earned. He bought petrol, cigarettes and a little beer and handed the rest over to my mother. I knew nothing about household bills.

For the three years at university I'd found casual work every holiday. I'd worked nights in an industrial bakery, with a disaffected immigrant workforce, including Whisky, the Polish giant, who loaded huge bread trolleys onto trucks throughout the night and sometimes slung them at his Pakistani supervisors. I'd wheeled barrows and mixed mortar for a one-legged Cockney bricklayer, who loved nothing more than to mock the university student for his clumsiness and then to thrash him at darts in the pub over pints of lunchtime Guinness. I'd beaten grouse on a Scottish estate, tramping in a long line through the mist and wet heather, flanked by gamekeepers, driving birds towards a line of butts and sometimes hearing the lead shot whistle past my skull. I'd worked in bars and shops and kitchens where I learned the simple truth that most work for most people was something to be endured, the grim unsatisfying price they paid to eat.

One Easter I painted the gutters on the accommodation building I lived in during the term, spending my days up a ladder that flexed when I climbed it and that I learned to move by bouncing it along the wall while still aloft because it was quicker than going down and coming back up again. At the end of three weeks my pay came in a sealed manila envelope. I took it to the toilet to open.

There was £120 in new £20 notes. I kissed them. Over those same weeks Tim and his lean friends were skiing in Austria. They sent me a postcard.

In the final term the big employers came scouting. Tim quickly secured a job with a multinational oil exploration company. Other friends aligned themselves with giant retailers and management consultancies and international accountancy firms. I didn't. It had never crossed my mind that I might enter the commercial world. I hoped to write but was only too aware of how bad everything I'd written was. Because Tim was a yachtsman I vaguely thought of crewing yachts around the world but did nothing to make it come about. I didn't want a career. I didn't aspire to wealth. I think I just thought something would happen.

'Here's just the job for you,' said Stan, a bluff lock forward, and he handed me the *Daily Telegraph*, folded to the personals column. 'English graduates wanted to teach English in Spain', followed by a postal address. I snorted. I didn't want to go to Spain, I didn't speak Spanish and above all I wasn't going to bloody teach. Fair enough, said Stan.

A fortnight later I got a letter from El Centro Ingles in Zaragoza inviting me to interview. In applying on my behalf Stan had even affixed a mugshot cut from the rugby team photo. 'It seemed just the job for you,' he said.

The interview was at a hotel near Marylebone station. As it happened I needed to go to London for a twenty-first party, so I hitched down the A10 then went to the interview to claim the train fare. The interviewer was a scrawny, middle-aged man with a beard of what looked like wire wool. Almost his first question was whether I played rugby, then what position I played – scrum half – then whether I could do a spiral pass – naturally – then whether I could demonstrate it, using – and I am not making this up – the glass paperweight on the desk. 'Good,' he said, when we'd passed the paperweight back and forth a few times, gingerly on my part, across the small hotel room, 'you could play for Spain.'

'Really?'

'Yes,' he said. 'I do.'

He seemed an improbable rugby international, but I knew myself to be a more improbable one still. I was under no illusions about my rugby. I liked the game, I was fit and strong and reasonably skilled, but I was a coward. Knowing I was easily intimidated somehow never stopped me being easily intimidated. I would will courage on myself, but none ever came.

I took the job. It was teaching, yes, but it was adult

evening classes rather than going back to school, and it had the consoling virtue of abroad. The salary on offer was in pesetas, hundreds of them to the pound. I worked hard to convince myself that the job was glamorous, an adventure.

The work began in October. That left me with a summer and a bit to fill. I spent the first three weeks of it on a folding chair beside the busier intersections of Brighton, counting cars for the council with a little clicker and sucking in the bitter fumes of necessity. Then, as if fate were keen to make a point, I got another teaching job.

Language Holidays was one of Roger Vellacott's many babies, in partnership with his wife, Dorita. They kept creating businesses because Roger kept having ideas. He was only ten years older than the teachers he employed but he seemed agelessly more mature. The son of a vicar, he'd sold helicopters in South America and done numerous other enviable ventures, but he still loved to sit up late with scotch and Benson & Hedges and argue over anything from grammar to god. In all discussion he was maddeningly rational. He was also generous with his laughter, and perhaps the kindest man I've known.

Villains and idiots are easy to paint. The kind are not. Roger took an unfeigned interest in others and had a gift for attracting the sort of people who interested him and then earning their loyalty. I worked three summers for Roger and Dorita and made friends who last to this day.

For Language Holidays they rented a prep school and filled it with European teenagers for the summer. It was sold to the teenagers as a holiday, to their parents as education. Many of the teenagers came year after year. The prep school that first year was outside Hastings and reminiscent of the ones I'd taken my under-nine-and-a-halfs to around Birmingham, a former country house with a warren of additions and outbuildings set in acres. It smelt of damp afternoons and floor polish and cabbage, and every cupboard seemed to house superannuated sports gear. I was given a room high up under the roof, former servants' quarters: a sloping ceiling, a single iron bedstead, a thin mattress, a battered chrome clothes rack on castors such as might display shirts in Marks & Spencer, bare floorboards, and a single unshaded low-wattage bulb. I lay on the bed that first afternoon and watched a squadron of tiny flies endlessly circling beneath the bulb. Every so often two orbits would intersect and there would be a brief frenzy of combat before the safe and pointless orbiting resumed.

A knock at the door and Mike Friend came in, grinning. And as I type this more than forty years later, Mike is half a mile away on the other side of Lyttelton. Swarthy, handsome, he was already an old hand at Language Holidays and had been all but adopted by Roger and Dorita. I warmed to him on the instant. He rendered life dramatic.

Only a few days later he burst into my room early in the morning in a medical panic.

'Joe, Joe,' he said, shaking me awake. 'You've got to look at my arse.'

He was serious. He'd noticed worms in the toilet bowl, had straddled a mirror to see if he could see them at source, as it were, and when that failed had come to me. When that failed he went to Dorita who proved both braver and kinder. Not only did she confirm the infestation, she also told him what to do about it.

An hour later, at the quiet village chemist's, Mike waited till it was busy before addressing the pharmacist. 'I've got worms,' he exclaimed for all the shop to hear. 'Hundreds of them crawling around my rectum.' Because making it theatre was the only way Mike knew to deal with it.

Everything for Mike was theatre. At the end of the first half of the summer we took forty kids to Heathrow to see them off. The first left early in the morning, the last late in the evening. I foresaw a long and tedious day at an airport. Mike foresaw a captive audience.

The pranks varied. The fishing gag in which Mike reeled me up a staircase and through a crowded restaurant before coshing me dead with a rolled-up newspaper drew applause from much of Terminal 2. The staged fight over a suitcase in the central concourse drew only the police. The kids took great pleasure in impeding them as we ran.

One afternoon Mike, Andy Johnson and I took all the kids up to London to see a matinee starring Tommy Steele. Once they were safely ushered into the theatre Andy and I snuck off to see *The Tin Drum* in the cinema opposite. We didn't tell Mike because he'd have wanted to come too. When we came out from the film it was to find the kids already milling on the pavement along with Mike and the theatre manager. The show had bored them and they'd thrown sweets. Tommy Steele refused to come out after the interval until our kids were removed. The manager was not happy. Without Andy and me there we'd broken some law about the ratio of students to adults. There was talk of legal action.

Back at school Andy and I went to Roger to tell him we were at fault. Roger heard us out. 'Thanks for the apology,' he said. 'How was the film?' You had to love him.

And while I'm on acts of kindness, Dorita saved my life that summer. I batted a wasp away from her daughter and was stung on the neck for my pains. Shortly afterwards I felt itchy and said I was going for a swim. Dorita announced she was taking me to hospital. I scoffed. She insisted. It was a half-hour drive. By the time we arrived my neck and head were so swollen I was struggling to breathe. The doctor injected adrenaline into my buttock. I continued to swell. 'You're going to feel a little excited,' he shouted into my swollen ear as he injected more adrenaline directly into a vein.

It was like running out onto Eden Park at the start of an All Blacks test. It was almost worth getting stung for. And the swelling shrank on the instant. Another hour and I was back at school with the sort of sagging, ravaged face I have now. Back then it tightened up within a day.

At the end of that summer I went hitching through France, a final fling before starting a life of work, though the main aim of the trip was to drop in on Fontainebleau, where Tim was due to start his own career. I kept a notebook of the trip; I have it still.

My first lift out of Dieppe was from an English man and wife in a plush Rover.

'You married?' asked the husband, as I got into the back seat.

His wife sat silent, head down, her hands folded on a map of France.

'If you want my advice, stay single. It's a trap, I tell you, the oldest bloody trap. That's why they make you take vows. Otherwise every bloke would be off within minutes.'

There was no levity in his voice, and he did not relent and his wife kept her head down and did not speak once. It was a long way to Rouen.

That night I pitched my little borrowed tent in a wood near Chartres. The police came by. 'Can I help you?' I said in my best A-level French.

'A quoi faire?' said the cop, and demanded my passport. They got on the radio for a bit, turning the passport over as they spoke as if there were some mystery to be found in it, then they drove away with it. It was a long bad hour before they returned. 'And you can't camp there,' they said, as a parting kindness. 'Privé.'

It was dark. I started to strike the tent, then changed my mind. I crawled into my sleeping bag fully dressed, ate a peach and some biscuits and didn't sleep. I was scared of returning cops, of an aggressive landowner, of some distant barking dogs. I wrote a note to my future self telling him never to romanticise travel. I woke at dawn sodden. It had rained and the tent had leaked. I rolled everything into my backpack in record time and ran down the road to warm up.

Outside Poitiers the next day a man stopped in a Renault 4 and asked me where I was headed.

'Angoulême,' I said.

'My mother's sick in Angoulême,' he said, 'get in.' As we drove south he told me all about his mother and her illness. When that subject dried up I tried him on others but he wasn't interested. We lapsed into silence. Just before Angoulême the main road curved away towards the south-west. A young couple were hitching. My driver stopped, asked them where they were heading. 'Bordeaux,' they said.

'My mother's sick in Bordeaux,' he said, 'get in.' He then told me to get out because I'd bored him. I walked into Angoulême. It was a hot day. I bought a bottle of lemonade and went to sit on a bench in a little park. A man was asleep on the other end of the bench, a huge dog on the ground beside him, the lead draped loosely over the man's wrist. I looked at the dog and then I looked again. It was a lion. It was that sort of a trip.

I swung down through the south of the country and then back up to Fontainebleau, south of Paris, arriving the day before Tim was due to get there. Just outside town I parked my tent in a forest clearing across from a semi-derelict caravan.

The following morning I was woken by a bass breathing, as if a large dog were sniffing at the edges of my tent. I lay still. The beast went around the side of the tent. With great caution I opened the zip and peered around the side. A wild boar, richly tusked, was exploring the edge of my tent where I had a little food stored. I zipped the tent back up. I held down the inside edge of the tent. The boar moved along a bit. I went along with it. We were separated only by nylon. My knuckles gripping the edge were white.

Eventually the beast seemed to lose interest and as far as I could tell it moved away but it was a while before I found the courage to unzip the tent again. Across the clearing a man was sitting on the steps of the caravan, feeding the boar by hand.

That afternoon I walked into town and there, parked just beyond a large metal street map of the centre of Fontainebleau, was Tim's low-slung orange Honda. I stepped out from behind the map and asked if I could help him. Few moments in my life have afforded me a more intense pleasure.

It was the first of many rendezvous with Tim over the next twenty years across a range of countries, continents even. What he made of me I didn't quite know, but I could never see or think of him without feeling what I

166

felt then, a gush of mental sunshine. I felt it again just the other day. I'd emailed him in London to ask if I should use his real name in this memoir or a pseudonym and when his reply came, when I saw his name pop up in the inbox, I felt a flutter of the heart, and saw him as I always see him, as he was then in France, tall, lean, in jeans, smiling. Yes, he said, as I'd been sure he would, I should use his real name, and, by the way, he'd just become a grandfather.

The following morning in Fontainebleau, hung over and weary of hitching, I spent the last of my money on a train back to London. Two English youths shared my compartment. 'That wasn't a holiday,' said one, 'it was a fucking endurance test.' Sitting in the corner with my little notebook I wrote it down.

In London I turned around in a day and caught a bus to Spain and adult life.

Chapter 21

I reached Zaragoza in the evening after a thirty-six-hour journey that ended with a slow hot train from Barcelona full of wailing babies and their black-eyed mothers. From a station pay phone I rang the number on my letter of appointment. A Spaniard answered, sounded displeased and hung up. I dialled again. The same man, further displeased. I tried a third time. The phone was off the hook.

I was unsure what to do. Then the thought arose, like a ship coming slowly over the horizon, that I'd been the victim of a hoax. I had never applied for this job. The interview had been an absurd thing where I had been both flattered and tempted, and where there had been very little mention of actual teaching. And now here I was in a city in north-east Spain, with a suitcase, £10, no job, no return ticket and no Spanish. Even as I gulped I found myself thinking this would one day make a story.

Exhausted from the journey, I curled up on a bench in the station only to be woken some hours later by somebody touching my hair. I opened my eyes to find half a dozen leprous faces within a foot or two of my own. When I jumped up the faces melted back into the shadows. They belonged, I later realised, to the drunk and the homeless who came to the station overnight for the warmth. They'd been studying me out of curiosity, there being no indigenous Spanish redheads, and no word, indeed, for red-headedness. El rubio, they used to call me, the blond one.

An elderly man was dialling a pay phone. 'Elizabeth,' he said, 'Elizabeth', then replaced the receiver. Feeling very much alone, I asked if he was English. 'Absolutely, old boy,' and together he and I sat up for the next few hours on Zaragoza railway station.

He was in his sixties. By profession he played poker, not as in today's televised tournaments, but in illegal gambling evenings held in private London houses. When he was flush, as now, he went hitchhiking around Europe, commandeering lifts with a furled umbrella. He followed no route, just went where the lifts took him, which was how he had fetched up in Zaragoza. His hobby was metal detecting, hunting for Roman coins, and he opened his travel bag to show me his detectorist kit, nestling among some neatly folded white underwear.

'Do you find many coins?'

'I've never found one,' he said.

Elizabeth, it transpired, was his ex-wife. He called her sometimes just to hear her voice answering.

I laid out my predicament. 'Oh, I shouldn't worry too much, old boy, if I were you,' he said, 'something will show up, you'll see.' And there was a quality about him, a buoyancy, a faith in fate, that did me good.

When the station cafeteria opened at dawn he bought me an omelette and a brandy. 'Good luck, old boy,' he said, 'you'll be just fine', and he shook my hand, then headed off into the rising sun, his travel bag in one hand, his umbrella tap-tapping on the pavement, going he knew not where. And, of course, I was just fine.

I found a station official who spoke French, explained my problem, showed her the address of my supposed employer and she pulled out the phone book and lo, I had a job again. The phone number had been one digit out. Two days later I was teaching.

El Centro Ingles was one of thousands like it all over Europe, schools that sold the hope of fluency in English. The trade was TEFL, teaching English as a foreign language, and the one qualification for being able to teach the language was being able to speak it. On the same principle, every car driver is a mechanic. The school occupied two floors of an apartment building in the central city. I slept there in a storage room my first few nights, then found a room in a flat in the industrial outskirts of the city a couple of miles away across the Ebro. My flatmates were a tiny combative Irish girl and a plump compliant English one.

New teachers received no instruction, other than being handed a spectacularly archaic textbook written by the man who had interviewed me and who ran the sister school in Madrid. I never used it. My immediate boss was Marc, who dressed sharply, spoke softly, was rumoured to have hepatitis and rarely came to work. The effective boss of the place was Thierri, the secretary, a Spanish woman in her late twenties, hard nosed but soft hearted, who, as was typical for the unwed, still lived with her parents. She allocated classes, took the money and dispensed advances on salary in cash from the till.

I generally taught one class in the morning, often a solitary university student desperate to improve, and then four or five classes in the evening, finishing at 10. Many of my classes were social, groups of housewives who came for the company and not for the subtleties of English auxiliary verbs. I learned Spanish more than they did English. And it suited me just fine. I liked the teaching. I liked making the women laugh. And I liked Zaragoza.

It was a city of three-quarters of a million people but you rarely saw a tourist. When Tim and two equally tall friends came to visit later in the year, my students told me they were in town before I knew myself. I spent a lot of time in and around the Basilica del Pilar, built beside the huge and muddy Ebro. Here was religion as I had never seen it. The entrance was lined with beggars showing off their deformities, sores and stumps. Some even then may have been victims of the civil war, which had ended forty years before. The victor, General Franco, was only recently dead. I met old women who refused to believe it.

Inside was a great ornate barn, cool and always busy with little ceremonies in side chapels, confessionals, people lighting candles, people praying, and the black cloth of the priests swishing with self-importance over the marble slabs. There were murals by Goya and relics in chests and no aliens but me.

The altar was a dazzle of gold and jewels, and at its heart the small stone pillar on which the Virgin Mary appeared to St James not long after the Crucifixion. At the back of the altar you could kneel and kiss the pillar's base. There was always a queue to do so, mostly women. I joined them once and as I knelt my first thought was that this was unhygienic and my second thought was how indicative my first thought was. This place was a fine long way from Hassocks.

Just around the corner stood the central market, where the toothless garlic seller sang the same chant day in day out – 'Tengo ajo, blanco como la leche' (I have garlic white as milk) – and where there was an aisle of offal, displays of intestines, sweetbreads, pizzles and rows of peeled and grinning goats' heads sold with or without brains, each with a little ring of fur left on the muzzle. And in charge of every offal stall a black-eyed Spanish girl with impeccable make-up.

I liked to wander in the city. I liked learning the language. I joined the only rugby club and we went down to Barcelona every weekend to play and laugh. I liked the little bars, the cheap beer, the rough wine, the tapas of olives and anchovies and the rich cold omelettes. Above all, I relished being far from home, responsible for my own fate. Exile suited me. And I had a typewriter.

In my last year at Queens' I'd written a dissertation on Evelyn Waugh – a 4000-word fan letter dressed up as objective criticism. To type it as required I'd borrowed a portable machine and been reluctant to return it. I found the pressing of the keys put a critical distance between myself and my own words. It sieved out some of the adolescent self. It made me write better.

My new typewriter was an altogether more impressive machine, a Spanish-made twenty-pound cast-iron matt-black office job that I'd found in a cupboard in the school and felt a fierce and immediate lust to own. Not daring to ask if I could take it away lest I be told no, I stayed late one night and stole it, lugging it up Avenida de Cataluña, its iron chassis scoring deep into my palms, to Calle de Felisa Galé and our flat on the eighth floor. I put it on a table at the window of my bedroom overlooking a crossroads and a parade of shops and a sister apartment block, the windows all net-curtained. I cleaned it and oiled it and used it every day. Its Spanishness was an added virtue, the letter ñ, the sexy inverted question mark.

I wrote letters. I wrote to everyone I had an address for. It was a form of publication, writing for a known audience of one, performing on paper, turning a life into words, wrapping it in an envelope and posting it off like a little bomb of self. It gave me such licence and such incentive to experiment. Writing to be read. Writing to record. But also to invent. To create something solid out of the flux of the impermanent.

It is hard to credit now how complete the severance was from all I knew. There was no internet, of course, no mobile phones. No one I knew had even a landline and an international call from a pay phone was unthinkably expensive. Mail was it. I felt as pleasingly far from England as Laurie Lee had in the 1930s. When I got letters back the airmail envelopes landed fat with promise but they rarely fulfilled it. Few of my friends were eager correspondents. But every letter that arrived was a chance for me to write another in reply. The form suited me. My letters were essays and experiments.

'Dear Paul,' one letter began, written at my window late at night having taught till 10 pm and then gone for beers in Gabby's bar in the Tubo, a writhing labyrinth of medieval streets, 'It is black out there and friendless'. And then, for the first time in my life, a story began to tell itself.

Paul never got the letter. For a week I came straight home from teaching each night eager to sit at the keyboard. I had always hoped to write. Now for the first time, I was writing. The story was called 'Mariel'. I took the name from a lithe young winger in the local rugby team. He was forever extending his medical studies at university in the hope that one day the authorities would abolish 'la mili', the compulsory military service. Because he knew that if he ever went into the army they'd crush him for being clever, for being pretty.

The protagonist of my story, El Jugador, was a performer, a public fighter and prisoner of the state, who, to cut a short story shorter, sacrificed himself for the younger Mariel. It was inexplicitly homoerotic. And it gave me hope.

Chapter 22

When Kingsley Amis visited Philip Larkin at the University of Leicester, he is said to have looked around the common room and said, 'Crikey, someone should do something with this lot.' The result was *Lucky Jim*. But Amis could have said the same about every common room I ever belonged to, including this little school in Zaragoza.

The longest-serving teacher was a stout young Englishman in his late twenties who had married a Spanish girl and whose sole ambition was to achieve a life of utter uneventfulness. When I first arrived in the staffroom he eyed me from behind his newspaper and for a couple of weeks maintained a cautious distance. Months later he explained that he'd left England owing £50 to the Leeds Permanent Building Society and whenever a new teacher arrived from the UK he was nervous that he or she might be 'from the Leeds'.

Some teachers had just walked in off the streets. One such was Aidan, an Australian who did his hair in Abba curls. The notion of Aidan trying to teach the workings of a language, even, or indeed especially, his own, was a worrying one. After living in Spain for six months he'd still barely got beyond please and thank you. Once he famously tried to order a beer for himself and a gin and tonic for his girlfriend. The barman cocked his head and asked him to repeat the order. He did so. The barman shrugged, laid six plates on the bar and put a doughnut on each one.

Another walk-in off the street was Edinburgh Dave, a painter and decorator, who would still have been painting and decorating Edinburgh and supporting the Hibernian Football Club had a young woman from the village of Fuentes de Ebro not gone on a study trip to Scotland. The moment he saw her he laid down his paintbrush and his previous life and he followed her when she returned to Spain. And though she did not encourage him, he persisted until she relented. Long before she did so, however, Dave ran out of money and sought refuge in the non-judgmental arms of El Centro Ingles, where he was able to impart his remarkable accent to a generation of Zaragozans.

And then there was Tanya from Cardiff. Her hair was a cascade of black ringlets. She laughed a lot. She looked good in dungarees. She'd known Sammy Barnes at university so there was an aura by association. And sometimes she would lay a hand on my forearm, which was cheating. I fell for her to a degree that made me think I might be straight.

It was a hopeless cause. Her taste was for brown-eyed, black-haired, honey-skinned Latin types, of which there was no local shortage. As a grey-eyed redhead who blistered at the sun's first touch I wasn't so much an outsider as a non-starter. But I strove to endear myself. For her birthday, after long deliberation, I gave her a little glass jewellery box that wasn't expensive but was still more than I could afford. I watched her face when she unwrapped it and knew the thud of failure. I wrote a story about her, or about my thwarted keenness for her, on my big black typewriter, but I knew as I typed it it lacked the emotional heft of 'Mariel'.

Tanya shared a flat with Big Paula and Little Paula. I learned more about womankind from them than I did from Tanya. They were just about the first women of my age I had had much to do with.

I was present when Big Paula received a letter from her boyfriend in England dumping her. She took the blow with what seemed aggressive cheerfulness. 'Come on, Joe,' she said, 'we're going shopping.' Currently in fashion were leather ankle boots with a folded top. I thought them hideous but was not about to say so. The first shop had nothing in Paula's size. Nor did the second. In the third shop the assistant kindly suggested we try the men's section. It was outside this shop that Big Paula fell apart, sobbing on my shoulder so violently that passers-by stopped to stare. Having no idea what to do I did nothing but hold her awkwardly. She calmed down in the end.

The other Paula, little Paula, enjoyed the role of confidante. She liked that I liked Tanya and liked hearing me speak of her and did her best to break it gently to me that it was the lost cause I already knew it to be. (Indeed I'd have struggled if it wasn't. Sighing aspirant suited me.) But when little Paula, in bed with some minor ailment, clasped her birdlike arms around my neck and pulled with a remarkable urgency, whether out of her own desire or out of sympathy for my plight, I pulled back, pulled away, resisted with a force that was both immediate and instinctive. Once again I knew in my heart that I was somehow, not by much, but with that not much making all the difference, queer.

Christmas Eve, and uniquely we went out for dinner at the school's expense. Even director Marc turned up, though he slid away early without anyone noticing.

Afterwards I went with Tanya and the Paulas to midnight mass, not in the basilica but in its gloomy medieval counterpart, La Seo. It was the first church service I had ever voluntarily attended and as the choir began to process out of the darkness towards the altar, carrying candles and singing something ancient that echoed under the vaulted ceiling, I began to shake, my teeth chattered like castanets. I was overcome by a sudden feverish weakness and I fell to the floor of cold stone flags.

Delirious, I was taken back to the girls' flat. They summoned a doctor who was Christmas drunk. He diagnosed food poisoning and plunged a needle fiercely into my backside and I spent Christmas and Boxing Day shitting and puking and having dreams flash across my mind like landscapes seen from a racing car. Three days later I pulled on a pair of jeans and they fell back down. Tanya and the Paulas went away to France and two days after, still weak as water but eager to make some use of the Christmas holiday, I walked out to the western edge of Zaragoza and stuck my thumb in the air. My first lift was from a priest in a little green Renault.

'A dónde vas?' he asked.

'Por allí,' I said, 'over there,' and I gestured vaguely to the whole of Spain. And so began a trip through Castille and León as far as Salamanca, where the Plaza Mayor remains my favourite piece of architecture in the world, and the hitching was easy and everything was suffused with a sense I have always enjoyed, of being small and alone in a large and arbitrary world. Standing by a road between Valladolid and Burgos, with a small bag and the clothes I was wearing and a few pesetas in my pocket, I liked being abroad, being beholden to no one. When, years later, I read Laurie Lee's account of walking through Spain as a young man, I recognised the whole of it.

Back in Zaragoza I had to find a new place to live. 'Grande cama buena,' said a small ad in the *Heraldo de Aragón*, 'Big good bed', followed by a price and a phone number. The room was in a boarding house of sorts, owned by an ancient couple. The one small window gave onto a dank internal well. No sun reached the room. The single bulb was always on. But the bed, as advertised, was vast. Apart from an old black wardrobe, and a side table on which I stood my monstrous typewriter, it was the only furniture. You had to edge around it. To be in the room was to be on the bed.

I shared a bathroom and kitchen with two Spanish girls who spent all day in housecoats washing and cleaning and fussing over their fat little spaniel, and a self-adoring pretty boy whose room was on the outside of the building. He would sit on his windowsill, feet up inside the frame, basking in the winter sun, and then follow it around the building to the kitchen where he'd do the same, silently watching me if I came in to make coffee.

A hunchbacked middle-aged woman came intermittently to change the sheets and it was she who one day told me the ancient landlords wanted to see me on a matter of some urgency. I found them in their parlour looking mournful. Without a word the wife held up a bed sheet, folded to reveal to best effect some blood stains. The rugby pitches of Barcelona were hard and dry. I had little skin on my knees. I offered to pay for the sheet. No, no, said the old wife, I would have to go. This was a respectable house. When I finally grasped what I was being charged with, much to their bewilderment I burst out laughing. The confusion was resolved by my rolling up my trouser legs.

I stayed three months in that dark little room before moving into a cheap and magnificently derelict fourth-floor flat with Edinburgh Dave. It was at the end of a tenement block, one half of which had been demolished. If you looked up from the street you could see wallpaper hanging off the outside end wall of the building, and darker patches where pictures had hung. That was the wall against which my bed lay. It had holes in it through which, as I lay for a siesta in the heat of the afternoon, I could drowsily watch the world.

Dave's romantic pursuit of his beloved had succeeded to the extent that he was finally invited to dinner at her parents' house in Fuentes de Ebro. To lend him moral support I joined him on the rattling country bus that took us to the village square, where storks nested on the church tower. The area was renowned for its onions, but not for its cosmopolitan nature. Dave was six foot something and I had flaming hair. Even as we stepped off the bus we were objects of scrutiny. Kids on bikes circled us, staring and giggling. In the bar on the corner of the square people came in just to observe us in mute curiosity.

When Dave went off to dinner I stayed in the bar and drank. Mid-evening the doors of the bar flew open. 'Dónde está el rubio?' boomed the new arrival, 'Where's the blond one?' He was maybe five foot tall and four foot wide and rocking-on-his-heels drunk. The patrons parted in silence to reveal me at the bar. Short-and-wide swayed towards me, came right in close so I could smell his breath, jabbed me in the chest with a stumpy forefinger and informed me that there were three things of importance in this life and three only: to smoke Ducados, to eat serrano ham and to be afraid of nothing. His message conveyed, he lay down and slept. Little children sat on him like a sofa.

Dave returned from his dinner aghast. In deference to his foreignness he'd been given steak and chips, but the rest of the family had had a goat's head each. 'And Joe,' he said in his rich Scots accent, 'do you know what the best bit of a goat's head is? It's the gums, Joe, the bloody gums. And you cannae get at the gums with a knife and fork. You have to pick the thing up and gnaw. Joe, I've just watched my beloved clashing teeth with a dead goat. I nearly called it off.'

I wasn't sure the extent to which I believed him, but he didn't call it off. By the time I left Spain that July he was officially engaged. He and I spent our last night together getting maudlin drunk. At the end of the evening, in a sodden stupor, Dave heaved his head off his chest and looked at me with bloodshot eyes. 'I love her, Joe,' he said.

'I know you do, Dave.'

'And I'm going to be hen-pecked to fuck.'

Chapter 23

I spent the summer in England, mainly London. It established a pattern that lasted through most of my twenties: working the academic year abroad, then returning for a month or two. Sometimes, as this first summer, I had to work, but on arrival back in the country, at Victoria or Heathrow, I'd go to a phone booth and pull out my little black address book, wondering where first to dig my spade into the past.

Most of the people I called and went to drink with, and whose sofas I slept on, were plain friends, people I knew from school or college or cricket and found congenial, but there were a few names charged with more electricity. When I dialled their numbers I did so with a nervous trembling of the fingers. When they answered the phone I'd get a wordless kick. When I was with them in the pub I stood an inch taller, was brighter, more garrulous, more alive and more devious.

However I might have dressed it up to myself with words, it was lust, an amoral energy, the first spur to action.

There was never any action. All the friends I fancied were straight. It was a friendship that ached only the one way, but that ache lent a lustre.

Carl was a year or so my junior and unconventionally beautiful, his features bunched into too small an area, giving him an endearing mock frown. Hair en brosse, medium height, narrow hipped, able but not brilliant, athletic but not outstandingly so, and wounded by circumstance, by a broken family and a lot of bad luck, he had a lost boy quality to him that cried out to be loved. Soon after I got back from Spain we met up in a pub in Great Portland Street and I recall that night and the following morning not for anything extraordinary, but because I wrote it out the next day, and though I have lost what I wrote, the act of writing seared it in the memory. I'd written because I'd been happy. Let it stand now for the hundreds of such nights and mornings during the summers of my twenties.

After the pub shut we ate huge doner kebabs, then took the Tube back to Carl's rented ground-floor flat. In the Tottenham Court Road station dirty little mice scampered in the valley between the rails, unperturbed by the deafening tonnage of train a foot above their heads. Carl lived somewhere south of the river. The late Tube was the province of drunks, aggressively singing, or stumbling with laughter, or suddenly alone and feeling ill, or just sleeping. Morden, the last stop on the Northern Line, was always thronged with taxis for those who'd slept through their station.

I woke earlyish the next morning on the sofa and it was every sofa that I slept on in those years – the dust in the coarse fabric, the cushion as pillow, the opened sleeping bag as blanket. I lay there a while, dry mouthed, rehearsing the events of the night before, checking for moments of embarrassment, finding none and dwelling on the pleasures of it, of having had Carl to myself, of having affirmed a friendship.

I made instant coffee in the miniature kitchen, drank it looking out over the dank back yard with walls of yellow London brick, smoked a cigarette, then made a coffee for Carl and knocked on the door of his bedroom, got no reply, pushed the door open and he wasn't there. Gone to work presumably, poor sod.

The bed was a scrambled mess. On the floor his clothes from last night, the jeans and boxer shorts unpeeled and stepped out of and still lying not quite flat, retaining some physical echo of Carl's flesh.

After I'd showered there was only the one towel, still cold and wet from Carl. I wrote a note of thanks and fondness and made to leave and found the front door locked. Properly and fully dead-locked, from the outside, presumably by Carl, hung over, unthinking, habitual.

It wasn't hard to shin up the six-foot wall of the back yard. On the other side was an identical back yard strewn with lurid plastic toys and in the kitchen window, straining a pot, an Indian woman. I waved and smiled. She looked impassively at me, holding the pot. Keeping her eye, smiling, trying hard to look like someone who wasn't doing what I was only too obviously doing, I dropped down into her yard. The woman disappeared from the window and reappeared at the back door. She was wearing a pinkish sari and had acquired a child on the hip. I began an explanation but she did not seem to understand and I indicated that I'd just like to pass through to the street beyond, and without smiling or speaking she led me through her kitchen and living room to the front door. 'Thank you,' I said and was let out into the street.

It was another of those moments of elation and illumination, of sudden clarity. As I emerged onto that little terraced street in Balham, perhaps, or Tooting, I had a sense of a world bright lit and limitlessly various,

189

and of myself as a free agent, a roving observer of all its pointless energy. I felt buoyant as a cork. It was partly a residual sexual charge, but also my utter anonymity there, in that street on that morning, and the fact that no one had a claim on me that day, that week, that summer even. I had money enough for the moment and a world to wander.

I headed north by the sun, through quiet and littered streets, knowing I must eventually meet the river. I stopped to eat at a café full of men with bellies and tattoos. Bacon, eggs, sausage, beans and fried bread. When I jammed the tip of a knife into the fried bread it shattered like glass.

Further on, thickly painted railings enclosed a scrap of public land, a parklet, a token nod to wilderness. Here were a few square yards of trodden-to-yellow grass, dotted with little tumuli of dog shit, and a small round pond, the colour of the tea I'd just drunk. And at 11 am on a weekday a dozen people were seated equidistantly around its rim like hours on a clock face, fishing. These were not bent-pin-and-worm kids but serious adult anglers. And what tackle they had: 14-foot fibreglass rods, Abu Garcia fixed-spool reels, swing-tip bite detectors, rod-rests with cradles of softened leather – hundreds of pounds' worth of gear.

190

Red Routemaster buses rumbled by a couple of rod-lengths away, drunks with cans of Strongbow roared on benches, old men limped past with defeated urban dogs, and these men – and a couple of women – seated on folding chairs, turned their backs on it all and their faces to the water and they fished for a few tatter-lipped tench and carp. There was something heroic about their abstraction, their seriousness. One man was in camouflage gear. Mid-morning, south London on a working day in the early 1980s and I felt good.

That summer I lost my straight virginity. And lost is the verb, rather than, say, shed. The signature note was inadvertence. I had almost nothing to do with it. The benefactress, if that is the word, was an Australian nurse whose name I don't think I ever learned.

At a party after cricket in a Hampshire village, late in the evening, and without preamble, she plucked me from beer and friends, took me by the hand and led me upstairs, but every room was occupied by the like-minded. So we tried the balmy summer garden, but every nook there was taken too. Undeterred, she marched us out of the gate and along the lane to the village church with its ancient graveyard and there, on a worn old tomb, she laid me down. To say I was a passive participant would be to overstate my contribution. But things passed off after a fashion.

As a kid I'd often thought that life on the far side of sex would be different in some way that I would discover only when I got there. Ah well. But on balance I was pleased to have had the veil ripped off one of life's little mysteries. And the venue couldn't have been bettered. Indeed even during the event I made a mental note to record the name on the headstone for the purpose of future story-telling, but I either forgot to do so or I forgot the name.

Chapter 24

Foyer Sonacotra was a cheap hostel in the town of Nancy in eastern France. There were separate wings for men and women. Almost no one in either wing was French. On my floor it was North African Arabs at one end and Vietnamese at the other, with me in the middle. The floor below was Turks. The directeur of the Foyer warned me always to lock my door, even if I only went across the corridor to the toilet. 'Toujours, vous m'entendez, toujours.' He was an unhappy man in an unhappy place. He spent most of his day in a sort of reception area fortified with steel mesh.

On my third day there I came back from a morning's teaching to find a woman on her knees with bucket and cloth washing blood out of the lift. An Algerian had cut his wrists and ridden the lift up and down while he waited to die. When he collapsed the lift stopped and the directeur hauled him out and he lived.

In the communal washrooms the toilet seats had all been broken off at the hinges. Beside each bald bowl of vitreous enamel were two scatters of ash, one from left-hand and one from right-hand smokers. I was a leftie. In the communal kitchen the huge fridge was divided into lockable compartments. I put a few cheap provisions in one on my first day: they were gone within hours. I bought a little padlock: it was snipped within hours. I bought a larger padlock: within a day someone had broken off the little door at the hinges.

The Vietnamese would descend on the kitchen en masse, cook a noisy communal meal and be gone in an hour. The Arabs hated them, seemed to view them as inferior, perhaps because they themselves were despised by the French at large. There were often rows and threats of violence. One night, late, voices rang in the corridor right outside my door, guttural Arab and high-pitched Vietnamese, and there were thuds against the wall. I stayed in my bed and tried to read but it was impossible to ignore, and I got up and opened the door a crack and there was an Arab with a knife facing off with a Vietnamese youth in a stained white vest holding what looked like the metal leg of a chair and behind each stood a mass of shouting supporters. I shut and locked the door. The fight took a while to resolve itself. But even when the noise subsided I couldn't sleep and I sat up on the bed with the two thin pillows rolled to support my back and I wrote a story in an exercise book of the squared paper that they favour in French schools.

The story was about sitting with Tim on a stone wall outside the Fitzwilliam Museum in Cambridge waiting for the daily tray of pork pies to appear in the window of the bakery opposite. The trick was to get one when it was still hot, before the jelly had congealed: the thick crust, the smoking meat, the running juices. It was a medieval pleasure. The story ends with Tim biting into a hot pork pie for the first time and meat juice running down his chin. It was writing as therapy. When I was done with it I slept. In the morning there were brown smears of blood on the corridor walls.

I'd found a job through the *Times Educational Supplement*, a weekly paper full of depressing articles about teaching, but plump with situations vacant. Just to read the international section of those ads made my guts dissolve. I sent my CV to the Bannon School of English in Nancy and was offered a job by return of post.

I knocked on the door of the school on a Sunday evening. After a summer in England I was broke and presumed that I'd be able to take an advance on my wages to get me through the first month. Madame

Bannon answered the door and soon disabused me of that little notion. She was a small, domineering woman who made it emphatically clear that she had no intention of advancing me any money or indeed of helping me in any way on that or any other Sunday evening, so good night. And she closed the door in my face.

I had a few francs in my pocket. It was dusk. The street was empty. My first thought was to give up on the job and hitch back to London and start again, and I might have done so had not the handle on my only bag been made of a ridged black plastic that cut into my hand. I bought some tomatoes and a packet of petit beurre biscuits, found a cheap room for the night and presented myself back at the Bannons' the following morning.

'Are you the fellow who tried to borrow money off my wife?' exclaimed Jim Bannon and he clapped me on the shoulder and flung his head back with a laugh that was part delight but mainly incredulity. I hardly ever saw him laugh again. He was a tall intelligent Northern Irishman with a weapons-grade temper.

When I explained that I was broke and had nowhere to live or means to support myself for the first month, he ordered his wife to arrange accommodation for me. She gave me a cheque made out to the Foyer Sonacotra for precisely one month's rent and she made it clear not only that I was lucky to get it but also that there was absolutely no more where that had come from.

The contract I'd signed forbade me to undertake any other work while I was in the employ of the Bannons, but I had to eat. Of the various jobs I found to bring in a little illicit cash, the one I was most proud of was translating into French the technical specifications for a sewage plant to be built in Saudi Arabia. I got 500 francs for that.

The school was Jim Bannon's baby. His wife administered it and dealt with the money. There was a timorous secretary called Mademoiselle Poisson whom Madame Bannon bullied. But Bannon was the reason for, and the genius of, the place. It was a central city apartment turned into classrooms. French companies were required to spend a proportion of their profits on the education of their employees. They came to Bannon to learn English for business.

The principle that underlay Bannon's pedagogical approach was that if you pronounced English words with a French accent you were unlikely ever to gain any fluency. If you pronounced, say, the English word carrot in the French manner, with the emphasis on the second syllable and a fully sounded o, then you were unlikely to understand an English speaker who put the emphasis on the first syllable and swallowed the second. All of which struck me, and still strikes me, as perfectly sound. But the aggression with which he put this principle into practice and which he encouraged his teachers to imitate was remarkable.

Faced with a new class of four or five executives, all of whom spoke respectable, if very French-sounding, English, he would keep them waiting on stools in the classroom while he paced the corridor outside, carrots in hand, muttering to himself and working up a temper. He would then burst into the classroom, thrust a carrot into the face of the nearest startled adult and bellow 'Wha's tha?' in his best Ulster accent. (It was his contention that Ulster spoke the purest English. He used to play his students tapes of Ian Paisley.)

He would repeat this pantomime, growing louder, angrier, redder in the face and fully audible in other classrooms, until one of his students found the courage to say something along the lines of 'Eet's a carrotte', to which Bannon would reply with spit-drenched violence, 'No *eet*'s not a fucking car*rotte*, ut's a *carr*ut. Okay, again. Wha's tha?'

The class lasted an hour, by the end of which, ideally, the assailed students would be capable of conducting, in a passable impression of a Belfast accent, the following two handy passages of dialogue:

What's that? It's a carrot.

What're those? They're carrots.

Bannon justified the aggressive intensity by the need, as he saw it, to shatter French complacency. You couldn't teach them to speak English well until you'd convinced them that they spoke it badly. Is there a term in psychology for adopting an approach that gratifies one's own nature and then justifying it intellectually?

Apart from Bannon my colleagues were all female. Three of them lodged for a while at Sonacotra. One evening the directeur came hurriedly to my room to beg me to come at once to the female wing, which I had never previously entered. One of 'les Anglaises' was in a bad way.

I found Sally in the washroom just beginning to come down from a state of hysterics. At its height, apparently, she had been ungovernable, thrashing her limbs and banging her head. By now she was just leaning against a wash basin, sweaty, drained and shivering. But then once or twice, as if remembering some awful grief, she threw back her head and made a noise I had never heard before and don't have a verb for. By way of an answer to my curiosity I was shown to a toilet cubicle. Curled in the bowl was what looked like a piece of irregular off-white string. Part of a tapeworm, apparently.

I went with Sally to the doctor's the next day as interpreter. The doctor, chain smoking, said she'd have got it from rare steak and prescribed some powders that, he said cheerfully, would be sure to kill off the rest of the family. I feared that when I passed this on in English Sally might kick off again but she just stared at me, then clasped her head in her hands and groaned.

My route to work each day took me over a canal in which one of the Vietnamese used to fish for tiny bleak and roach, squatting in the Asian manner for what seemed like hours. Sometimes he would look up at me as I crossed the bridge and would hold my gaze without a flicker. I liked that. From there I passed through the Pépinière, an ornamental park at the heart of which stood a little municipal zoo where the principal exhibit was a solitary bear. It paced a concrete landscape all day looking out into the park across a moat on which buns floated and sandwiches and general litter. It seemed the saddest animal on earth.

While I paid off my English debt I lived on very little, breakfasting on bread and jam, lunching on bread and cheese, dining on bread and eggs, and plugging the gaps with cigarettes. The only indulgence was Saturday when I played rugby for the local ASPTT, the post office sporting club. It wasn't much of a team but then I wasn't much of a player. It suited me. After a game the whole team would go out for a meal. I would make an excuse, dash back to Sonacotra to fry some eggs, then rejoin the team later for beer and misadventure.

A few weeks into this routine one of the backs, Dédé, a trainee accountant, took me aside after a game and urged me to join them for dinner. I made some excuse. 'Look,' he said, and he put a hand on my shoulder, 'if it's a problem of ...' and here he made the international money sign, rubbing finger and thumb, 'I will pay.' I had to turn away. I find kindness overwhelming, always have. But I accepted Dédé's generosity only once.

By Christmas I was solvent and keen to escape Sonacotra. A colleague, Andrea, feistily affable, got wind of a flat going cheap just yards from the central square, Place Stanislas. The reason for the cheapness soon became clear. The place had not been lived in for years and all three rooms were packed with vast quantities of evidently stolen goods – boxes of new boots and of pornography in plastic wrappers, new car tyres, a dozen guitars. It took us a whole weekend to lug everything out and into the landlord's van to be taken we didn't know where. But the landlord, a softly spoken Algerian who ostensibly ran a picture-framing business from the ground-floor shop, neglected to tell his contacts that he was shifting his operation. Often I'd come down in the morning to find that overnight half a dozen brand-new bicycles had arrived in the corridor, or twenty boxes of shampoo, or once and startlingly, a huge hydraulic ramp that stayed for months, presumably because no one could find a way to get it back out again.

But it was a great flat. A large front room with tall metal shutters gave out onto rue Stanislas. It was from those very French windows that we watched the celebrations of the election of François Mitterrand. He was the first left-wing president of France in a generation and Nancy was a left-wing town. The party went all night, cars driving around and around Place Stanislas with their horns blaring and drunks with flags leaning perilously out of their windows, and a little old woman walked beaming through the crowds handing out roses. It struck me then and it strikes me again now that I have never had reason to celebrate an election, nor yet to mourn one. Government has rarely impinged on me, and war, never. Lucky's the word.

Once a week a driver collected me and drove me twenty miles out of town to a vast foundry where I was hired to give an hour's English lesson to the CEO. He

202

was a gruff, fat, funny curmudgeon who smoked Gitanes Maïs, lighting each one from the stub of its predecessor. He'd been a child during the war and at any reference to Germans or Germany he would turn to his metal waste bin and spit a great smoker's gob into it that made it ring like a bell. (Similar, spitting aside, was my mother's reaction to the German golfer Bernard Langer. Blond haired, ice-eyed, he was the distilled essence of Luftwaffe pilot. Though she liked watching golf, and acknowledged that Langer was no doubt a splendid young man, she couldn't bear the sight of him.)

Andrea slept in an alcove off the front room. I had a smaller room behind. Across the stairway was a shower, toilet and rudimentary kitchen. But the great virtue of the place was its location and it became a multinational drop-in centre. I taught a lot of evening classes. I would come in at nine or ten at night to find a dozen people in the front room, all of whom had brought booze, conducting conversations in three or four languages.

Guillaume was a regular, a French dentistry student, easy-going, tall and spectacularly handsome, though he was not, I thought, my type. One morning I went into the front room to fetch a book. Andrea was still asleep in her alcove, and sleeping with her, his naked back to the room, an arm draped over her, was Guillaume. And the jolt I felt at the sight of his long bare back was a mule-kick of lust, was a sickening surprise.

But I was not in love and these were good days, highly social, and if sometimes there were too many people in the flat and I wanted peace, I would hitch out into the surrounding country to be on my own. I bought an orange portable typewriter and made good copies of stories I'd written here and in Spain and packed them off to little literary magazines in England that I had never read. Back they all came, some with dismissive comments, some with a printed rejection slip, most with no comment at all. And rightly so. Apart from 'Mariel', I knew they were no good and I had no idea how to make them better.

So I was left in the usual quandary. I could teach, and there were always jobs to be had. But there were also a couple of young women at Bannons who'd taught a year or so in each of seven or eight countries and who planned to carry on being peripatetic into middle age. I saw in them a warning of how easily I could delude myself that by moving on I was getting somewhere. Geography was not the answer, but I didn't know what was.

At the end of the academic year there was a joyless farewell party for the departing staff, which was pretty well all of us. Madame Bannon made little secret of her disdain for us. Bannon made none at all. He emerged from his office, tapped the table for silence, coolly but emphatically informed us that we were the worst mob of teachers he had employed in the twenty years he'd been running the school and that he would be delighted to see us all gone, and returned to his office and shut the door.

On my own behalf I am rarely combative, but I followed him and knocked on the door and told him I'd worked hard for him and that I reckoned I'd taught well and that I resented being told I hadn't.

'Oh, I didn't mean you,' said Bannon. 'I was talking about the others.'

Thanks a lot, I didn't bother to say, but I did ask for a reference. He wrote me a belter.

Chapter 25

In September 1981, I hitched up to Sheffield to begin a one-year teaching course in physical education. The fact still surprises me.

Gaining a teaching qualification seems an odd way of getting out of teaching. And I assuredly did not want to teach PE. Of my two PE teachers at school one had a prognathous jaw and liked to raise little boys onto tiptoes by gripping the tuft of hair just in front of their ears and lifting. The other seemed perpetually delighted by his own good looks and, when not preening in front of a mirror, could be relied on to have one hand, and not infrequently both, plunged down the front of his trackpants.

But I had been turned down for a job in Greece that I'd been so certain of getting I had applied for no others. Then a friend suggested a postgraduate certificate in education as something to fall back on should I ever need it. I found I quite fancied a year of student indolence, drinking and sport, and I could get a grant to cover course and living costs, there being, then as now, a shortage of teachers. Since I hoped never to teach, it really didn't matter what subject I majored in. And then, by the time I applied for a last-minute place, there was only Sheffield left, so that was that.

Sheffield, my father's home town, immediately struck me as alien. Here were the terraced houses of the nineteenth century and the overlay of grime from heavy industry. The local language was barely mine. 'Get thee sat down,' said the first PE teacher to speak to me. Reet was an adverb, as in 'he were reet funny'. The standard greeting was 'All right?' – pronounced 'aw-rai'. And the standard reply was 'All right', pronounced the same way but with slightly different intonation. Get that intonation fractionally wrong, however, and 'Oh aye,' your interlocutor would say, 'what's up?' I felt more abroad than when abroad.

I shared a terraced house straight out of Coronation Street with two history students who kept different hours to me so all was well. In the shared kitchen I cooked exactly the same evening meal for months on end – bacon, egg, boiled potatoes and carrots – but the great virtue of the place was the loft. It had been converted into the best bathroom I have ever had the use of: peak-roofed, airy, splendidly lit by windows set into the roof that granted views of the scudding northern sky, inducing elevated thoughts while shitting and rousing songs while showering.

There were ten of us on the PE course. We spent the day in tracksuits being taught the rudiments of a variety of sports. The director of the course was a former British discus champion. There was a lot of emphasis on the discus. In the pool I learned that nine out of ten white males floated and that I was the tenth. Then I was sent out on teaching practice to a colliery town some miles from Sheffield.

The first morning on the bus I was sitting upstairs in my tracksuit, smoking. As we neared the school, kids got on. Some of the older ones came upstairs and sat at the back and lit cigarettes. Of course I did nothing. It was the same the next morning. On about the fourth morning one of the smokers pointed me out to his mates. Though I hadn't taught any of them they must have seen me about the school. But they still lit up. The following morning I came downstairs before their stop. They saw me on the lower deck and grinned. Did I want a lifetime of such compromises, such defeats?

From an upstairs window of the gym block I looked down on the music room, a single Portakabin-type building. One morning I watched unobserved the only music teacher, a chubby man, close to retirement, with a horseshoe of white hair, take a fifth form class. He arrived late. The kids were milling outside and paid him no attention. With great difficulty he began the process of ushering them into the room, his arms spread wide like a shepherd in a dog trial. But even as he ushered them in, a fire escape door on the other side of the room burst open and those who'd gone in came out again. This all took ten minutes to resolve. With the kids finally corralled and both doors closed, he put some classical music on the record player and that was that for the second half of the class. I could see only the back row through a window. They were paying exactly as much attention to the music as you would expect. A boy and girl necked for twenty minutes uninterrupted. When the bell rang both doors erupted. I saw the teacher in the staffroom ten minutes later taking morning tea. He seemed untroubled, blithe.

The PE department was run by just the sort of man you'd imagine, iron muscled, local, serious and not to be crossed. One snowy morning he sent the fourth form on a recognised cross-country route – over the playing field, around a circuit in the woods and then back. I offered to run with them. 'Nay lad,' he said, 'we'll take our time', and we had a cup of coffee before jogging off together across the playing field and into the adjacent wood. 'Watch this,' he said and went a few yards off the trail and shook a small tree. Boys fell out.

Later that week he was away for a morning and asked if I'd take his fifth form class. 'And don't take any shit,' he said, and I am not going to try to reproduce that sentence phonetically. It had several more than six syllables. There were times in Yorkshire when I felt it was still Danelaw.

It was snowy again. The gym was occupied by another class. I announced that we were going to play five-a-side football on the tennis courts. My charges were less than impressed. Their legs, as I led them out of the changing rooms, were the whitest things on earth. There were two tennis courts, the nets taken down for the winter. Snow had begun to settle. I organised two teams for one court, got a game of sorts going, turned around and the other half of the class had fled. I ran around the end of the nearest building, couldn't see them, came back and the rest had gone too. I'd lost a class. Soon a teacher appeared at the PE office holding a youth by the collar. 'One of thine?' he said. He'd found him under the woodwork block. The kid's legs had gone from white to blueish.

PE wasn't hard to teach but it was rarely satisfying. Sometimes I'd get a buzz from some child acquiring a skill, doing a head-stand, say, or a vault of sorts, or, yes, making the discus fly, but not often. Most of the time it was just organising and supervising games and trying to make sure the fat boy wasn't humiliated.

I played a little rugby for the university. The rugby was good, the after-match games startling. One particular evening in the West End the whole team was obliged to take part in an elaborate drinking game, with forfeits along the way for mistakes but with the penalty for the ultimate loser being to drink a glass of urine, which was neither his, nor fresh. To be precise it was the captain's from first thing that morning, saved for the purpose. Foresight, you see. I managed not to lose. And also not to stay long enough to see the penalty enforced.

There was a rugby tour to France. I didn't go. The captain did, despite being on crutches with a broken leg. His first act on arrival in Paris was to find a telephone and cancel all the matches. Rugby wasn't to be allowed to get in the way of a rugby tour.

The cricket was more congenial, good hard northern cricket played on large cold grounds to a high standard. Lunch at every game was pie and chips, the pie like molten magma, the chips crinkle-cut and pale as Nordic legs. But we were a fine team of happy lads and had the wicketkeeper not missed the simplest of all possible stumpings in the last over of the semi-final, we would probably have won the national university competition for 1981. But the boys forgave me.

While I was at Sheffield, Mike Friend was at college on the other side of the Pennines doing a degree in the performing arts. One requirement was that he should write, direct and perform in a play. The directing and performing were not a problem, but Mike could no more write a play than he could fly. So he came to me.

Each summer at Language Holidays I'd written a play for Mike to stage. They weren't high literature – the best of them was entitled *Princess Di Meets the Killer Gorilla* – but I found them easy to write because there was no self in them. That there might have been something to learn from this never occurred to me. What I did learn from them was the difference between Mike's mind and mine. Where I thought in words on paper, he thought in images on stage. I was verbal, he visual. It remains true today.

So I wrote a play for Mike's degree and posted it to him, one scene at a time, and then a month or two later I went to see it performed. It was set in a rugby changing room. *'Against the Head,'* said the programme, 'by Mike Friend.' I tried not to feel peeved. Afterwards the examiners in the audience summoned Mike for a viva on 'the writing process'.

'What do I say?' asked Mike.

'You'll find something,' I said and he did of course. Later that evening I declined the invitation to write a dissertation for him. But he soon found someone else to do it. In the end I think there were five of us who owned a part of Mike's degree. His highest mark was for some costume designs. These had been done on the kitchen table in not very long at all by Roger and Dorita's ten-year-old son.

That New Year's Eve Roger and Dorita gave a party. Around midnight Mike found a realistic police officer's cap in a cupboard and suggested we go out and stop traffic. It was typical of Roger to point out that impersonating a police officer was a jailable offence and then to suggest where best to do it.

I was drunk enough to want to go first. Mike hid in the hedge. I put on the cap and a long black coat, stepped into the road and raised a hand. The car stopped about ten yards short of me, an elderly couple framed in the windscreen. I went to the driver's window, taking care to speak over the top of the car. When I asked the old boy at the wheel if he'd been drinking he stammered his denial. When he reached into the inside pocket of his jacket for his wallet and driving licence, he tore the lining. The intoxicant nature of power.

'Thank you, sir,' I said, handing the licence back. 'Drive safely now.'

'Thank you, officer,' he said and I could hear Mike giggling.

A Volvo. Again I stepped out and raised a hand. The car kept coming. I held my ground and the car stopped at my feet.

'You seemed a little reluctant to stop, sir.'

'Yes,' said the driver, a man in middle age. 'It was your tennis shoes.'

I passed the coat and hat to Mike. He at least had black shoes on. He stepped out in front of a Ford Escort. It accelerated, swerved around him, then fifty yards further on it screamed to a halt, all the doors opened, and half a dozen youths got out and ran, leaving the car on the side of the road with the lights on, doors open, radio blaring and engine running. Mike and I went back to Roger's.

In the final term at Sheffield, and with a sense of being drawn in by the whirlpool that I'd been circling for years but with no idea how to steer away from it, I applied for several teaching jobs in England. Two asked me for interviews, the first an independent school in the greenest depths of Dorset. There was a village nearby with a double-barrelled name straight out of Hardy. It was early summer and the land was as lush as Eden and the roads shrank to lanes with green walls and the rest of the world seemed a thousand miles away.

My interviewers were a jaunty young headmaster, full of plans and ambition for the school he had recently come to, and a grizzled deputy head, full of resentment for the jaunty young headmaster. And, since the head took a shine to me, for me.

A deferential youth showed me around the school and grounds. The first eleven were playing and I could see immediately how it would be. I would grow to care whether they won or not, would get involved in the fates of the kids, would know the school politics, would become a fixture in the place, one of the live-in bachelor masters whose life was the school and whose reward was the influence he could bring to bear on an endlessly self-renewing tide of adolescents, with him alone becoming older in a sea of youth. I knew it would suit my nature. And I knew, even as I was being interviewed, that I would be offered the job. And that it would be happily fatal to accept. And that I would accept. And that would be that. Claimed by the whirlpool.

The other interview was at a smaller independent school in Kent. The headmaster had that speech impediment of 'w' for 'r' that seems to exist only among the posh. 'Tell me, Mr Bennett, what do you think of teaching dwama?'

'Oh, I think drama is so good for the children, the freedom to inhabit other skins and to imagine', or some similar guff.

'No, no, Mr Bennett, gwama, English gwama. Do you believe in teaching English gwama?'

I did not get that job. I did get the one in Dorset. And then I got a phone call. That in itself was remarkable. Since leaving home I hadn't once had a phone number, hadn't once even lived in a house with a phone in it. This call found me playing basketball in the gym at the University Athletics Centre. A secretary came running in excitedly, calling my name. There was a gentleman on the line from British Columbia.

I thought British Columbia was in South America. I ran to the phone in her office.

'John Fenter here, Mr Bennett, Vancouver Island, British Columbia. Patrice Lemais speaks very highly of you. I'd like to offer you a job.'

Well now, Patrice. I had never expected to see or hear from him again. He had been a gauche and gangly member of the rugby club in Nancy, always eager, always present at matches and at after-match events, but somehow never getting around to actually playing because of a series of unspecified injuries. But he was affable and generous and he liked to be with me because he was doing an American literature course at the local university and he loved to practise his parodically accented English. In exchange for some university meal vouchers I once rewrote an essay of his on the short stories of Sherwood Anderson, though naturally without reading any Sherwood Anderson. The essay scored a C. The French professor's main complaint was that my English was unidiomatic.

Patrice had sometimes spoken of a brother in Vancouver and hinted at his intention of joining him there one day, but it was just Patrice talking. Now, however, it seemed he'd not only gone to Canada and got a job at a school on Vancouver Island but he'd also persuaded a headmaster to offer me a job sight unseen.

I was sorry it wasn't South America. I had never wanted to go to North America and though I saw Canada as less brazen than the States, I still suspected it of the same sort of cat-hat and Mack-truck absence of irony. But the offer plucked me at the last moment from the deep green Charybdis of Dorset. 'Thank you very much, Mr Fenter,' I said.

Chapter 26

I was sent out into the quad to greet the new boarders. A car drew up, an Oldsmobile or some such, the size of a small garden. The driver's window wound down electronically, which was still impressive in 1982, and a large, moustachioed American father looked me up and down. 'You here take care of my son,' he said, 'while I go find a teacher.'

'Of course,' I said. I was twenty-five. I shaved every third day.

I had rooms in the senior boarding house in exchange for doing duties there. The grade eleven floor I was ostensibly responsible for was packed with Mexicans who maintained the national stereotype of charming indolence. We soon arrived at a pact of mutual non-molestation. I didn't expect them to do much in the way of work and they didn't expect me to do much in the way of interfering with their social life.

The boarding house was the empire of Reg Douglas, a rotund Welshman nearing retirement, a former naval officer and a fellow of the Royal Society – for what reason I was never able to find out, but FRS was appended to his every signature. He was emotionally volatile and a teacher of French to the slow. To teach next door to Reg was to be drowned out: 'Je donne, tu donnes, il donne,' thumping the desk with the rhythm and having his class follow suit, 'nous donnons, vous donnez, ils donnent.'

Reg belonged to a generation of teachers who were being increasingly eased out of the classroom and into ancillary roles. The person doing the easing was John Fenter, the headmaster, brought in to bring the school up to date. Nominally Reg was one of two deputy heads. Practically he was on the descent into irrelevance and he felt it keenly. Several times I met Reg straight out of a meeting with the head and I feared for his heart. His face would be purple. He spluttered abuse, rich with naval slang, his thumbs twanging his braces, his head shaking with disbelief.

But the gale would blow over fast. Reg was essentially a bluff, kind and hearty man. That Easter, when he learned that I was joining a school trip to Mexico, he made a point of taking me aside after breakfast. He clasped my forearm, looked theatrically over his shoulder and said in a stage whisper, 'Don't fuck the whores.'

Reg was the only man in the world to enjoy a fire drill. Legally you were required to hold one a year. Reg held two a term. Perhaps they reminded him of naval discipline. He'd set off the thunderous alarm at five in the morning, then stand at the foot of the stairs with a stopwatch. 'Come on,' he'd bellow at the freshly woken Mexicans, 'come on, you hairy dogs.'

The first time the alarm went off it took me a while to register what was going on. By the time I blundered down with a towel around my waist it was to find the others already assembled in the dark.

'There you are, Mr Bennett. Everyone accounted for on your floor and all doors and windows shut?'

'Yes, Mr Douglas.'

'Right,' said Reg. 'One minute fifty-eight. We can and will do better.'

On the way back up I met two of my charming Mexicans on their way down.

Where Reg was transparent, John Fenter was enigmatic. He had done a job of resurrection on a school in central Canada and had been brought to the west coast to work the same magic. He had plans in abundance but rarely showed them. Almost his first act, only a couple of years before I arrived, had been to introduce girls, an act which met apparently with fierce resistance from the old boys, one of whom demanded to know, at an extraordinary meeting of their association, who was going to beat them.

John Fenter could seem remote but he knew what went on in the school by the simple and wise expedient of talking to the kids. And he knew the potency of praise. If the rugby team you coached won a tournament a little handwritten note would appear in your pigeonhole. Fentergrams, the staff called them, and they were publicly mocked but privately relished, because oddly enough what works with kids works with adults too. Indeed, if you teach for a bit it soon becomes clear that the only substantial difference between teachers and pupils is that teachers are better actors.

In the staffroom one morning Fenter announced that he intended for the school to become rich. Increasingly thereafter he would appear at public events accompanied by one or more frail and elderly widows. These women did not always seem to be entirely sure of what was going on but they clearly enjoyed the attention being paid to them. The upshot was that several of them wrote the school into their wills. One who promised a quarter of a million had the headmaster's residence on campus renamed after her while she still breathed, with space discreetly left on the plaque for the word 'memorial' to be added when the sad day came.

But the sad day refused to come. Fenter recruited perhaps a dozen of these women, and they proved far sturdier than their appearance suggested. The problem, if one can call it that, seemed to be that the school gave them an interest and a purpose. One, in her nineties, when on a tour of the boarding facilities and shown the basement laundry, exclaimed that she had worked in a laundry as a young woman in Saskatchewan during the First World War and could think of nothing she'd like better than to do so again. So the frail old dear came in to fold sheets a couple of mornings a week and it did her no end of good. In the whole time I was there none of the widows died. Paradise indefinitely postponed.

It was a good place to teach. Schools have cycles and this school under John Fenter was in good shape. The roll was strong, the staff, by and large, collegial, and the kids, by and large, lovely.

At Sheffield I had let a student dentist practise on me. She had not been deft. I happened to say as much to a member of the school board of governors who, in the great tradition of selfless governance, just happened to have a kid at the school, and also just happened to be a dentist. His appraisal of the state of my mouth took a while. I needed several replacement fillings, a couple of root canals, a gold tooth or two, the cost of all of which amounted to the price of a serviceable second-hand car.

'No worries,' I said, 'I've got insurance.'

'I know,' he said.

And it wasn't just the insurance that the school supplied. The school housed and fed me. I had no expenses except cigarettes and they were cheap. And I was far better paid than I had ever been. At the local mall, I could actually buy stuff. It was a novelty.

But such money as I spent I spent largely on dining with Clem. Married to a quiet and clever editor of children's books, and father of a seven-year-old daughter who played the harp, Clem was six foot four, bearded like a Viking, perpetually broke and head of English. More pertinently, he was the man who made me laugh more than any other ever.

When a governmental inspector once asked to see Clem's lesson plans, Clem said no. The inspector reminded Clem that he was empowered by the relevant authorities etc. Again Clem refused, 'But,' he added by way of appeasement, 'I'll show you where I make them if you like.' 'Very well,' said the inspector, 'lead on,' and Clem led him smartly down the corridor, across the quad, up the steps into the Challoner Building, along the corridor on the second floor then stopped about a yard from his classroom door and said, 'Normally about here.'

On a Friday or Saturday night he'd pick me up from school and drive me to some hushed expensive restaurant in Oak Bay where we would start with cocktails, move on to wine, have every course from soup to cheese and finish with a string of Irish coffees topped with whipped cream from an aerosol can, and I would pay for all of it, and it never crossed my mind to mind. I was paying to laugh. I laughed so much it hurt. I laughed so much other diners asked to be moved away.

The meal would be a monologue from Clem, some of it rehearsed, but most of it fresh, found as he went. It was a torrent of vitriol, his subjects anything and everything from his father's dementia to the shortcomings of our colleagues. Never before or since have I known such unhesitating verbal fluency, of which the base ingredients were disdain, hyperbole, judgment, cruelty and relish. It was magnificent in its rudeness, its honesty, its joyous malice. I wanted to bottle it. It was Clem's art, his great creative act. You could see him surprising and delighting himself with the skewering felicity of his invective.

Clem fancied himself as a poet and showed me poems from time to time, and I was polite about them but they were tame. They had none of the force of his comic rants, the rants that welled from a deep rich vein, that were an unalloyed expression of self as only the best art is.

I sensed even then that it was partly compensation. Clem was dissatisfied. He wanted more money, more recognition of his talent. His heart was not quite in teaching. He was good for the brightest kids, those who could absorb a lecture. They went on to university with a sense of the history of western thought that would have put them years ahead of their peers. But Clem had less patience for the ordinary and the dull, for those who found it hard to learn by listening. And he was haunted, I think, as many men are, by the one great question: 'Is that it?'

Clem had friends who'd started businesses, written books, made money. He spoke of them wistfully and often. Some years later, after I'd gone elsewhere and Clem was well into his forties, that climacteric decade when men become afraid not of dying but of dying without something for their tombstone, Clem quit teaching. He pulled on his sixteen-piece suit and he went to Vancouver to act as golden-tongued charmer for an outfit whose nature and purpose I never quite grasped. I don't know how it turned out, but Clem is now long since retired.

His occasional emails are gnomic, cryptic, sometimes still blindingly funny.

Victoria was said to be the most English city outside England, and American tourists routinely arrived with a walletful of pounds. It wasn't remotely English. The roads were too straight and wide, the street numbers ran into thousands, and like all of North America it was built around the car. I still did not drive.

It was a ten-minute walk from the school to Hillside Mall. I would rarely see anyone else on foot. The houses were single storeyed, surrounded by lawns without fences or hedges, and eerie in their suburban silence. Shopping malls are now commonplace the world over but Hillside was the first I'd seen. To reach it on foot I had to cross its colossal car park, a moat of asphalt, at the heart of which stood the cheaply built barn, with its constant light and temperature, its synthetic floors that owed nothing to nature, and the limitless range of goods. Once you were inside there was never a door you had to pass through to reach those goods. They were there alongside you, already in your life, there to be taken, to fulfil the North American duty of consumption. I found it part seductive, part repellent, but always alien.

In the Christmas holidays of 1982, I borrowed a coat that had a hood trimmed with wolverine fur, and hitched from Vancouver up through the Rockies to Calgary. There in the cold I caught the train across the prairies. As we pulled into Moose Jaw, Saskatchewan, half a day later, the guard announced that the outside temperature was minus forty. I pulled the wolverine tight around my face, stepped out onto the platform and spat, having heard that the spittle would freeze in mid-air and land with a tinkle, like glass. It didn't. But by the time I laid a boot on it, it was stone.

The streets of Moose Jaw were just compacted ice on which the locals drove in spiked tyres as though they were summer asphalt. Cars were plugged in at night to little stanchions to prevent their engines freezing solid. If you laid skin on metal the skin stayed. And if you walked to the edge of Moose Jaw at night, beyond the last of the street lights, and you looked to the horizon, you could make out the headlight beams of cars spearing up from beyond the curvature of the earth.

On Christmas Eve I moved on. The station waiting room was the size of a school gymnasium heated by a boiler the size of a horse. I was the only passenger. The ticket clerk told me the train was 'fruz up in the Hat', Medicine Hat, just to the west. I spent the day there waiting. In the evening the clerk urged me to get some sleep. He'd wake me, he said, if the train came.

He woke me at five on Christmas morning. The train wasn't coming, but they'd sent a bus for me. It was a fifty-seater. I was the only passenger. I sat at the back. The man drove me all through Christmas Day across the limitless prairies, white and featureless for hours through which I drowsed and he did not. Our shared communion of Christmas ended 400 miles later at Winnipeg. I watched from the frozen sidewalk as he turned the bus around.

It was when hitching somewhere beyond Winnipeg a day or two later, beside a highway that stretched to the horizon in both directions, that I watched a car approach for minutes, growing from a dot to a blob to a windscreen and a single male driver who applied the brakes and slowed to offer me a lift. And as he did so I dropped my thumb and I looked down and he drove slowly past and then accelerated fiercely away. How could I have explained it to him? It was the vastness of the prairie, the limitless snow, the dome of the sky and only me under it, all of it conspiring to induce the sense of insignificance that I relish, of knowing for a fact that nothing matters. It comes only in moments and I wanted a little more.

Vastness, in the end, was what Canada offered. The country clung to the forty-ninth parallel and looked to the south, but with the whole of the Arctic on its back, a billion square miles of trees and lakes and rock and snow and silence.

In New Brunswick on the morning of New Year's Day 1983 I turned around and headed back west, and got the longest lift of my life, to just short of Toronto. My driver was a chain-smoking merchant seaman with a range of nervous tics and a cough so seismic that it would fling him against the back of the seat then hunch him breathless, wheezing, over the steering wheel as we veered across lanes. His car was an ancient battered thing with a ripped vinyl bench seat. Each time we stopped for gas he tried to top up the oil but he shook so much that it streamed over the engine block.

He put me in charge of the radio. If I found an audible station he would tire of it within minutes. And he talked about sex, told improbable stories of sex, asked me about sex. And he drove me over a thousand kilometres. About two in the morning we reached Belleville, where I was going to visit an English friend. I said to drop me at a motel. He said he'd come in and have a shower before going on his way. I could hardly say no

We had to wake the motelier. I explained I wanted a single room, but that my companion would be taking a shower before carrying on his way, if that was all right.

The motelier said he'd do me a twin room for the same price in case my companion wanted a lie-down. I could hardly say no. While he showered I got into bed. The bangs and crashes from the bathroom were startling. I heard the door open. I lay on my side, face to the wall, curled foetally with my fists clenched. He stopped moving. I could hear his breathing at the foot of the bed. Come one step closer, I thought, and well, I doubt I looked very asleep. He stood there far too long. And then he gave a sort of wheeze and he was gone. Relief was soon followed by guilt.

He'd used every towel in the bathroom. The floor was awash. There was blood on the basin and the mirror and the walls.

Chapter 27

After a year in Canada I resigned. It was all too easy, too seductive. I could sense the school putting its smothering arms around me and urging me to stay and grow rich. I liked my boss, the kids and most of my colleagues. I was becoming invested in the place. There was none of the oppressive class warfare of the UK, none of the snobbery of the private school, nor the antagonism of the state. If I was going to teach, I would not do better. But I felt I was not done yet. There had to be something bolder out there, which only fear was stopping me finding. Always do, said Emerson, what you're afraid to do. Wise counsel, though I have rarely been brave enough to act on it.

So I went to see John Fenter and resigned. He put up a flattering fight but I enjoyed denying him, insisting on leaving. Three weeks later, in the last week of the school year, he called me back to his office. The teacher running the middle-school boarding house had decided to take a sabbatical. Would I do the job for a year? He'd halve my teaching load and double my salary. Just for the one year. Just as a kindness to him, John Fenter, just to get him out of a hole. Had I known then, as I learned later, that he'd dug the hole for just this purpose, I would still have accepted.

My new empire was the top two floors of the original school building. My colleagues christened it Toy Town. Up there I was nominally in loco parentis to fifty of so boys aged between twelve and fifteen. I was twenty-six. I had little idea what to do. By way of assistance I had two resident tutors, one a university psychology student, and the other a middle-aged Englishman who was also the first fifteen coach. The son of a rural vicar, he kept his watch on English time, flew back to England on the first day of every major holiday and returned on the last day, and he guarded his privacy with such ferocity that he denied owning a phone.

I had a bedroom and a sitting room on the top floor overlooking the playing field, with a bathroom down the corridor. My door was pretty well perpetually open and some kids took advantage of that and others didn't, and from the intensity of the contact I learned, or at least confirmed, quite a bit about myself, and even more about my charges. At the end of each term I had to write a report on each boy and I spent a long time doing so. It wasn't an academic or sporting report, but a comment on character and behaviour, an effort to distil in words just who and how these children were. And it was to be sent to their parents. It found it an engrossing exercise.

'Give me the child until he is seven' runs the minatory Jesuit motto. I don't know if seven is the actual cut-off, but certainly by the time they get to secondary school character is settled. The gloomy, the joyous, the gregarious, the abstemious, the hermitic, the miserly and all the rest of the catalogue are themselves already and ever more shall be so.

You can ease their lives, teach them things, make them laugh and make them think, but by the age of eleven, and probably much earlier, the leopard is spotted. So the notion that schools mould character, that they form the young into well-rounded thoughtful adults or whatever, the standard guff of every school prospectus since time began, is so much guff. As a later colleague put it, secondary school is essentially a pipe: what goes in one end comes out the other.

Consider your own contemporaries at secondary school. As the years passed and the school exerted its influence, did the bullies become kind, the timid brave, the quiet noisy, or did they all just become more thoroughly themselves and confirm the impressions you had of them on first acquaintance? School remains a good thing for any number of reasons, but let us not pretend it forms character.

One lad came to my study every evening with his toothbrush and sat and brushed his teeth in silence and listened to other kids tell stories of their day and then went on his way to bed. Another stayed one evening till every other kid had gone and then sat on in silence while I was marking essays and when I'd finished I said I thought he probably ought to be going to bed and he said 'My mum's got MS.' He went on to tell me how she had deteriorated over the years, going from plateau to plateau, but always down, and that now she was confined to a wheelchair. And when he'd finished telling me he just got up and went to bed.

And now I start to think of those kids, dozens of them come flooding back. There was a bully who was expelled for buying what turned out to be talcum powder from a downtown dealer. I wasn't sad to see him go.

Another boy was arrested for shoplifting pornography. He was a strange child, pallid, sly and hard to warm to. When I arrived at the police station the duty sergeant fetched him from a holding cell and gave him a graphic warning of where any future offending would take him. The lad, thirteen years old, stood looking at the floor, saying nothing, showing no emotion. In the taxi on the way back to school he continued to say nothing. I thought I'd wait for him to speak first. Eventually, as we turned back in through the school gates, he did. 'I come from a broken home,' he said.

The porn baron of the house was a lad from Hong Kong, perpetually bottom of every class he took and with a narrow and barely comprehensible grasp of English, except for his specialist area of reading. Once after lights out I overheard him regaling the darkened dormitory with a fluent fantasy of blue-veined pendulous breasts, with every 'r' and every 'l' transposed.

And then there was Roly, the plump, spoilt son of a gung-ho oil man and some discarded former wife. Halfway through his first term a dormitory inspection revealed that Roly, instead of sending his shirts to be washed, had stuffed them into drawers and under his mattress and then ordered new ones from the school suppliers. I made him carry each used shirt separately to the basement laundry from his second-floor dorm. I found him an hour later collapsed on the stairs and feared momentarily that he was dead.

His dad rang just before one holiday and told me to tell Roly to pack for all climates. They were going around the world. 'Venice,' said Roly at the start of the next term when I asked him where he'd liked best. It had the best video games.

There was briefly a craze in the house for mini-death by hyperventilation. A kid would stand with his back to a wall, breathe in rapidly a few dozen times, then another kid would lean his weight against the first boy's chest until he passed out and slid to the floor. The loss of consciousness lasted only a few seconds but it was startling to watch. I insisted on having a go and saw such a rush of images as I fell that as soon as I came to I wanted to go again. I told the story at dinner that evening in the dining hall. The school doctor happened to be there. He took me aside to advise me with some vigour to ban the practice under threat of expulsion, and to forbid the kids to mention it had ever happened. I did.

A headmaster once told me that the two things that mattered in a boarding school were the food and the hot water. I'd add a third: the teaching. Kids like to be taught well and they will tell you if they're not. You're not supposed to listen to complaints about your colleagues but I always did, partly for instruction but mainly for pleasure. I was rarely surprised. It's not hard to know who the good teachers are.

I think, for example, of Bill, a maths teacher who claimed not to sleep. Of a night he'd just lie on his back and be. He coached the senior basketball team and during a game he'd be volcanic with emotion, stomping the sideline, kicking the bleachers and subjecting the referees to a tirade that if repeated in the street would have got him arrested. Away from the gym he was as genial as you could wish, a great and generous laugher, and endlessly patient with the slower kids. In other words, Bill cared and he didn't pretend to be other than he was, and those two qualities, it seems to me, are the indispensable ingredients of teaching well.

Colin taught drama and seemed incapable of anger or unkindness. Precise of speech, bright of eye, generous and appreciative of others, both in class and out, he could not be ruffled even when directing the annual school musical. And he was deaf as a stone.

As in every staffroom I've known, however, there was a bullshitter. Is he – and it's always a he – unique to the teaching profession or is he to be found elsewhere, the man who feels compelled to convince you he has done all things and knows all things about all things?

I was trying to resolve a dispute between kids in my boarding house over a scuba gauge. 'What you got there, Joe?' asked Denis Farmer.

I said I needed to find out if the gauge was broken or not. 'Give it to me,' he said. 'I'll soon tell you.'

I hadn't known, but should have guessed, that scuba diving would be another of his inexhaustible areas of expertise.

He turned the thing over a few times, then declared that with this particular brand it could be hard to tell. 'I'll just ring Frank.'

'Frank?'

'Yeah, Frank White, best scuba man in town. Old friend.'

He dialled: 'Hello, is Frank there please? ... Ah Frank, didn't recognise you. Denis here ... no, no, Denis Farmer ... no, no, Denis Farmer from ... well, anyway, Frank ...'

But know-alls are brazen. He put the phone down at the end of the call unabashed.

There was also an Iago on staff, a stabber in the back, a spreader of malicious rumour, though in my innocence it took me a long time to recognise him as such. Overall, however, it was a happy school, as good a place to teach as I have known.

When I moved into the boarding house a sad old Lebanese maths teacher told me matter-of-factly that the building was haunted. Had he seen the ghost himself? 'Oh yes,' he said, 'it sat on the end of my bed.'

At the end of my first term I was alone there. The kids had all gone in an hour or two, and the English rugby coach had flown back to England. The building was eighty years old. It creaked and groaned. Without the constant noise of kids you noticed air currents, suddenly banged doors. I found the stairs unnerving, the corridors worse.

That first evening I was in my study around dusk when there was a sudden sharp report like a rifle shot. It seemed to come from the sash window that looked out on a huge old cedar and beyond that the playing fields. I put my head out the window. As I did so the phone rang. I went to answer it, then was suddenly scared and let it ring. I closed the window, drew the curtains, locked the door. The phone stopped ringing. Then it rang again. I didn't dare to answer it.

I sat and listened to the noises of the house. The place seemed alive. I heard footfalls. It was a long evening. My bathroom was down the corridor. I didn't dare make the journey and pissed in the grey metal waste bin. It leaked. And I, housemaster, in loco parentis to fifty charges, lone adventurer, citizen of the globe, got into bed and hugged myself. The next day I took a ferry to Seattle and did not come back till the day before the start of term.

Chapter 28

I had put off going to see the States out of indifference born of prejudice. What I thought I knew of the States I didn't like. Even as a child I hadn't thrilled, as others had, to the sight of a huge American car on a little English road.

Waugh's *The Loved One* was my Bible of things American. When Aimee Thanatagenos said, 'Dad lost his money in religion', I snorted. When Waugh described Americans as 'exiles, uprooted, and doomed to sterility', I nodded and committed the phrase to memory. I viewed the US as a culture without substance or permanence, a shallow place of two dimensions as opposed to the rich and resonant three of old Europe.

I had three weeks. I took the ferry to Seattle, a bus out of the city and then went to hitch south down State Highway 5. No one seemed to mind. Occasional cop cars slowed and drove curiously past but they did not stop.

It's forty years ago. My overriding memory is of size. The distances, the pick-up trucks, the tyres on the pick-up trucks, the freight vehicles, the freight trains, the supermarkets, the redwood trees, the blue-jeaned arses and the plaid-shirted bellies – it was all just big. The breakfasts too. The calorific value of a short stack of buckwheat pancakes, smeared with whipped butter and drenched in imitation maple syrup, would keep me going till dinner. But I regularly saw men and women order a tall stack, five or more pancakes, with syrup, and banana, and blueberries, and a side of bacon, a flitch of bacon.

In the course of thumbing several thousand miles in Britain and Europe I had never once been invited to stay at someone's house. In the course of a few days in Washington and Oregon I was invited half a dozen times. I turned them all down out of English reserve and a reluctance to be beholden, but was overwhelmed by the kindness and by the intense interest in that most engrossing of subjects, me. It is wrong to generalise on so small a sample, of course, but the Americans who gave me lifts seemed generous, happy and rich.

There was one exception. A very fat man with a very slow drawl in a very big truck told me shortly after I'd climbed aboard that he'd once had cause to kill a hitchhiker. But he soon forgot about it and gave me a good long lift.

While idling in downtown Portland, I was approached by a young woman with blinding teeth who invited me to undergo a psychological profile. At the office she led me to, she gave me a multi-choice questionnaire so long and hypothetical that I soon grew bored and ticked answers at random. Nevertheless I handed it over for her to feed into her organisation's computer – a novelty at the time and one that she made much of, though the beast was in another room and I did not get to see it. While the machine digested my answers and sat in judgment on my psyche, she left me with books to browse, all in lurid sci-fi jackets and impenetrably written by an author I hadn't heard of.

She returned with a long face and news to match. The computer adjudged me to be in a dire psychological state. I would be lucky to make thirty. Depression loomed and most probably suicide. Fortunately, however, there was help at hand in the form of Dianetics, a programme for mental health devised by the author I hadn't heard of. His name: L. Ron Hubbard, founder of Scientology.

This was the America I hoped to find.

When I crossed over the border into anything-goes California the first cop stopped and told me, in emphatic terms, to go catch a Greyhound bus like any other bum. Would he be so kind as to give me a lift to the bus station? He patted his holster.

If you didn't have a car in the States you were by definition an outsider. The Greyhound buses were gatherings of oddballs with strange packages and obscure purpose. There were about six people on the first bus I caught. One of them, heavily bearded, watched me come down the aisle, then followed and sat beside me. He was a Vietnam vet, and a Marxist Buddhist.

'You know when you talk to some people you get a tingling feeling? That's them walking in your mind ... I can hear plants scream. That's why vegetarians are a bunch of horse crap ... Jesus lived in England with the druids for five years. That's a fact.'

Eventually he fell asleep. I did too. I woke to find him all over me, smothering my face with kisses, arms gathering me in. He was a big man. When I'd finally fought him off he pretended he'd been dreaming and went blithely back to sleep.

We arrived in San Francisco in a storm so fierce it closed the Golden Gate Bridge shortly after we crossed it. The bridge's stanchions had been rattling, the driver fighting to keep the bus in lane. Downtown that evening, in a street that was a canyon of high-rise office blocks, there was a dancing cloud of hats about two storeys up, all of them held and flung around by some strange effect of the wind. The same wind snatched a notebook from my hand and smacked it into a wall twenty feet away. I took refuge in a bar where an Irishman, very drunk, spent an hour telling me how he'd left Ireland with nothing and made good, then dug through the pockets of his overcoat in search of money for more Bushmills and pulled out a wad of food stamps.

My only contacts in the States were an elderly couple, both real estate agents, who were tenuously related to my mother's family. They had come to England once and my mother had shown them around a bit and they had insisted that if ever I was in Los Angeles I was to look them up. I arrived at the Greyhound bus station in downtown LA late on Christmas Eve and went to the gents. A man followed me in and while I was pissing he undid his fly and waved his dick at me. I had to push past him to get out.

The street outside was poorly lit. I was some way along before I realised it was lined with sleepers. As I walked past with my backpack I sensed people stirring, eyeing me, assessing. Otherwise there was no one around and nothing open. I found an unvandalised payphone and rang my distant relatives. They were horrified to learn that I was downtown after dark. I was to return immediately to the bus station where they would come to pluck me from what would otherwise be a certain mugging and probable death.

An hour later I was sitting in the plushest car I had ever known, being driven along twelve-lane elevated freeways through an unrelievedly urban landscape for thirty miles or more to Orange County, where the live-in Mexican maid had already prepared the guest room for me and I was to stay just as long as I wished. When I woke the next morning there was a stocking at the foot of my bed. Inside it a pocket knife, an electronic calculator, a couple of T-shirts.

We drove for Christmas lunch to a brand-new hotel built in a parody Tudor style with turrets and a deliberate lean and low beams and a little duck pond out the front. My hosts were trying to make me feel at home. They could not have been kinder or more generous. They pressed me to let them know what sights I wanted to see in Los Angeles – Venice Beach, perhaps, Disneyland, Hollywood Boulevard?

I wanted to see only Forest Lawn, the cemetery on which Evelyn Waugh based his Whispering Glades in *The Loved One*. My hosts were disconcerted. But I explained that an English author had written a famous book about the place and off we went on Boxing Day. The place looked like a golf course of the dead, and all of it accessible by car. I left my hosts to drive around while I went about on foot.

Waugh had barely exaggerated. A plaque in the first building I entered announced that I was standing in front of the world's largest oil painting. Elsewhere, at one of the replicas of European churches, the voice of what might have been a nightingale was emerging insistently and repeatedly from a low box hedge. I fossicked in the hedge to find the speaker and a bird flew out.

I caught back up with my hosts and found them enchanted, surprised that they had not heard of this place, and already planning to visit again. So much to see, they said, and all so beautiful.

From Los Angeles I went inland. All cities are just camps on the skin of the earth but nowhere is that more obvious than in Vegas. Turn the lights off and the desert would reclaim it in a week. There were slot machines in the Greyhound bus station. There were slot machines in the foyer of my motel. There were slot machines in the only grocery store I could find.

In a place of blinding desert light, of searing desert sun, life took place in artificial light and air-conditioning. Inside the huge hotels it was impossible to tell night from day. They never closed, the temperature never varied, the machines were never turned off, the playing cards never stopped flipping. If you gambled, drinks were free. You tipped the short-skirted waitresses with chips. When someone somewhere won a jackpot the noise of cascading coins, of tumbling erotic wealth, was broadcast throughout the building. Every hotel served a buffet, all day, all night and all you could eat for three or four dollars, right there in the middle of a desert that could suck you dry and kill you in a day.

Men played the tables, women the machines. The men smoked and drank and strove to show no feelings. The women, their children grown up, their husbands unsatisfactory, sat slumped on stools feeding coins into their machine as if it were some giant neon pet. Hours went by. Days. People responding to simple stimuli as predictably as creatures of a single cell. I drank it in, then went north.

Salt Lake City wasn't much different. The Vegas barons and the Mormon church have both grown rich from the delusion that the universe cares. Temple Square is the heart of Mormonism, where all its holiest buildings stand. In the tabernacle I watched a guide park his gaggle of tourists at the back of the building, march the hundred yards or so to the other end, mount the stage, ask for silence and drop a readily audible pin. In the basement of the same building I found a larger bank of toilets than I had ever seen, hundreds of stalls and urinals, all of them gleaming, deserted and overseen by a battery of swivelling security cameras.

The temple proper was out of bounds to unbelievers, but there was a lavish visitor centre. A diorama, like a giant aquarium, contained the life-sized figure of the religion's founding father, Joseph Smith. He was on his knees praying for guidance, when lo, the angel Moroni appeared unto him, and a bright light filled the aquarium. It was Moroni who led Smith to the golden tablets from which Smith went on to translate the Book of Mormon. I asked a guide what happened to the golden tablets. 'They were taken back,' he said.

Lining the staircase of the visitor centre were oil paintings of the various prophets and saints of the Mormon church, most of them biblical characters in robes and sandals standing in stony places but looking a whole lot whiter than any Middle Eastern Arab. The last portrait was of Spencer W. Kimball in collar, tie and serious spectacles, he being a banker and the current president of the church.

A dome on the top floor housed a marble Christ, several times life size, whose arms ended in plastic bags. Only that morning, said the guide sadly, 'a foreign male, suffering from a psychiatric disorder', had climbed up Jesus unexpectedly and smashed his hands off with a mallet.

Salt Lake City, with its bars that would sell you a tonic but not a gin, seemed no place to spend New Year's Eve. I caught a Greyhound to the first town of any size in the next state. In a shop window right beside the bus station was a prominent display of T-shirts. 'Twin Falls, Idaho, isn't the end of the world,' they announced, 'but you can see it from here.'

I found only two bars open. The first was empty, the second was Herman's Tavern, with a barman called Ben and a morose clientele. I played several games of pool with a woman so cross-eyed it was hard not to stare and harder still to know whether she was staring back. She thrashed me. Midnight passed without comment. Ten minutes later Ben wished everyone a Happy New Year and was told to fuck off. About one o'clock I made to leave and was asked where the fuck I was going so early. So I stayed and drank more beer and played more pool, but no one cheered up. Next morning, in the diner next door to Herman's Tavern, Ben the barman was asleep at one end of the counter and the cross-eyed woman was cooking the hash browns and eggs. She made no sign of recognising me.

My one surprise from three weeks on the road in the States was the overwhelming generosity of ordinary Americans, their open-hearted friendliness. That aside, I had my prejudices pleasantly confirmed. It was a place dedicated to making a buck. It wasn't strong on irony. Religion was more undisguisedly a business than it was elsewhere. And the whole country felt founded on the triumph of appearance over reality, of hope over truth. All of which I had previously got from Evelyn Waugh, my favourite bigot. You find what you look for.

Chapter 29

Six thousand pounds. I had six thousand English pounds. It was an unimaginable sum, inexhaustible. There was years of living in it, years of living without working. Cushioned by it, I would sit down and write a novel, and thus I'd forge the life I wanted rather than one that obliged me to work against my will, to set an alarm clock, to wear a tie. The year was 1985. I was twenty-eight.

I'd done three cheerful years in Canada, loveless but industrious, immersed in the kids I taught and in particular in those who lived in the boarding house, for whose welfare I was, astonishingly, responsible. It could easily become my life. It suited my nature. So I resigned again and this time stuck to it.

'Where are you going to go?' asked the kid who cleaned his teeth in my room each evening.

I said I'd go back to England for a bit but after that, who knew?

He prodded a canvas map of the world on the wall of my room. 'Go there,' he said. It was Madagascar.

'I'll send you a postcard,' I said.

'Promise?'

'Promise.'

And I want to tell him that I tried. I made several overtures to the Embassy of the Malagasy Republic, as it then was, in London, and even went twice to knock on their door, but they were unforthcoming. The closest I got to the place was an old man I met at a cricket club who'd lived on the island when it was still a French colony. He said it was overrun with wild cattle. If you wanted fresh meat you just stepped out your back door and shot one.

The first thing I did after landing at Heathrow was to buy a typewriter for fifty quid. This was the infancy of word-processing and the machine was mildly futuristic. Its one virtue was that it could hold a small chunk of text in editable electronic form before committing it to paper. But it was awkward to use and it required thermally sensitive paper, which was expensive, hard to find and even harder to store because it turned black if creased or warmed. The machine was a crock. But it wasn't to blame for anything. It was just the external expression of my self-delusion. I wanted to write but I didn't know how.

I'd started a novel in Canada, writing in brown ink on foolscap. I've still got it. The story is set in Canada, oddly enough, in an independent school, oddly enough, and features an expatriate Englishman in his twenties who has fallen into teaching against his will. Anything else you want to know? But it isn't the poverty of imagination that haunts me most. It's the poverty of the prose. Despite having an English degree, I had no idea how to rev the engine of the language. I didn't know the craft. I didn't know there was a craft.

I spent the summer travelling the country, visiting friends, playing cricket and drinking beer. The friends were prospering. They had bought flats, even houses. Instead of a dusty sofa I now got a pull-out sofa bed with sheets and duvet, or even a bed in a bedroom proper. There were wives, too, or live-in girlfriends, increasingly responsible jobs, and less enthusiasm for the pub. My friends were settling down.

Summer became autumn. The cricket season ended. I found myself spending more and more time at Peter and Andy's flat in North London. They were improbable flatmates. Peter had been brought up Catholic on a Hampshire council estate. His musical talent had taken him to good schools, an Oxford organ scholarship and a posh accent. Funny, ironic, sharp of wit, he was working as a freelance journalist, forever dashing out late at night to chase a story in his left-hand-drive Lancia. Tall and bespectacled, Peter seemed never to have a girlfriend and I suspected, wrongly, that he was gay.

Andy, on the other hand, was the son of a drunken publican. He'd been to drama school and was now trying to find a niche in the profession, testing out the notoriously difficult stand-up circuit. Andy was volatile, generous, wounded and handsome. He had beautiful girlfriends who were every bit as volatile as he, ashtray-throwers, impossible-demand-makers.

Neither Andy nor Peter was settled then. Neither had any idea where they would be in a couple of years. I felt at home with them and they let me doss on the sofa in their front room for weeks at a time writing nothing.

It was on that sofa after a party of sorts that another nurse simply got into bed with me, for a night of almost incessant drowsy coupling, with the drowsiness acting for me as a disinhibitor. We woke in the late morning to an empty flat. And I couldn't talk to her. I made her toast and coffee but I was incapable of smiling at her, at this woman with whom I'd spent the night. I could sense and understand her bewilderment. I hated myself for it but I longed for her to go. I did not regret the sex but I found myself powerless to behave with warmth or simple kindness. She soon went. And I can now only uselessly offer the apology I couldn't manage at the time.

It was also in that front room, when the lights came on at four at the end of another year, that I watched a black and white movie in which a train pulled into Budapest railway station amid clouds of steam and I felt a surge of lust for elsewhere. Neither Andy nor Peter was interested so I rang Keith, a cricketing friend, posh, idle and lucid of mind. 'Why not?' he said, typically.

A month later when our train pulled in at Budapest it was the first time for either of us behind what was then still the Iron Curtain. Keith, as dedicated a capitalist as ever drew breath, had brought along half a dozen pairs of Levi's jeans. Every citizen of the Eastern Bloc was said to be willing to give their life savings for a pair of Levi's though at the same time they were said not to have much in the way of life savings.

There were no clouds of steam but Budapest station was suitably vast, cold and grey. As we walked down the platform with our bags, Keith, who had already shown signs of nervousness, looked over his shoulder and said, 'We're being followed.'

I laughed.

'I'm serious. We being followed by a man in a raincoat and a pork pie hat.'

I stopped and turned. Behind us, also stopped, was a man in a raincoat, its collar turned up, and a pork pie hat. We walked on. He walked on.

On the main concourse I turned again and the man was still behind us, impassive of face. I walked towards him to see what he would do. He stood his ground. I stopped in front of him.

'Americans?' he said. His voice was old and feeble but tinged with faint hope. His English was just about good enough to convey the idea that he wanted to rent us a room for $5 a night.

It was two long bus rides to the outskirts of the city and rows of Soviet tower blocks. His flat was on the fifth floor of the third block. The lift was broken. The one room of any size in his flat was filled with a grand piano. On it stood emblems of the west – crayoned flags of European countries, an empty bottle of Head and Shoulders shampoo, a cardboard McDonald's hat. He showed us photographs from the war. One was of him as a young soldier sitting on a toppled statue. 'Lenin,' he said, stabbing at the photo with his finger, 'is Lenin', and he giggled like a schoolboy. It was the only time I saw him happy.

He begged us to go with him to the police station to register our presence but we refused. When we set out the next morning to catch a bus back into the city he tagged along uninvited, sat a few seats away and followed us when we got off but we picked up the pace and soon lost him. We paid him treble what he'd asked for the room. When, after two nights, we said we would be moving on he wept.

Hungary in the mid-1980s was a staging post between the west and the Soviet bloc. Czechoslovakia was the full deal. In Bratislava we sought a room in a large, seemingly deserted, state-run hotel but the woman at reception, as stony-faced as you could wish, told us the place was full. We gestured to the empty lobby, the absence of guests. She was unmoved.

There was little to do. We sat in bars drinking the cheap beer, eating sausages and playing chess. No one paid us any attention. I have an overriding mental image of greyness and oppression. When we left the country some days later we had a surplus of the local crowns. Even at the official exchange rates a few dollars made you rich and there was nothing to buy.

It was illegal to take Czech crowns out of the country. At the hotel we were told we could only change them back at the border. At the border we were told we should have changed them at the hotel. Kafka might have written the script. The machine-gun-toting border guards clearly expected to get the cash, but there was a little shop at the border station selling chocolates and vodka and we bought most of their stock. We then moved on to customs, where all we'd just bought was confiscated by the same border guards. Kafka would have admired that too. We got back to London still with six pairs of Levi's.

The money leaked away. I wrote nothing. Deciding that the problem was a lack of a room of my own I found a flat in Isleworth, in south-west London, a basement bedsit with a toilet in the back yard festooned with spider webs and a resident population of drowsy non-biting mosquitoes. I would sit needlessly long in there, despite the cold, catching mosquitoes between finger and thumb and pitching them into a web to see what unfolded – whether the mosquito would escape, whether the spider would bother – anything rather than face the crappy typewriter and the miserable truth that I was going nowhere and spectacularly not doing what I had told myself, and others, I would do.

The need to earn money became a dot on the horizon and grew larger depressingly soon. I did some relief teaching at a comprehensive school in West London. It was not a joyous place. Absenteeism was rife among both staff and kids. There was work for me any day I wanted.

At the end of morning break and lunchtime it was the job of the deputy head, an ambitious young man in a shiny blue suit, to go around the staffroom chivvying teachers out of their corners and dispatching them down the corridors. One woman I used to accompany on the long march would stop outside her classroom door and cross herself. The noise from the other side of the door sounded like a riot in progress. She breathed deeply and went in. The riot intensified.

Good teaching is personal. Relief teaching isn't. You don't know the kids nor they you. You are warder not mentor. Confrontation is common, as is indifference. Both disconcert me. I'm tempted to trace it back to fear of my father, but I doubt that it's his fault.

I remember only two actual classes. One was fifth form economics. They had a work sheet to complete on the subject of insurance. I sat at the front desk and thought of Lawrence's poem written in similar circumstances. And I grew so bored and disconsolate that I told them to stop working – redundantly in most cases – and invented an insurance scenario in which I reversed my car out of a garage and into a car that was illegally parked across the drive and asked what my insurance liability was. And a scrawny kid with a shock of white hair piped up on the instant to say it depended on whether I had third party or comprehensive and then he had an intense and improbably well-informed argument with a fat kid who clearly hated him and it turned out that they both had fathers in the motor trade. The scrawny kid told me afterwards it had been a great class.

The other was an English lesson where I was more at home. Again it was the fifth form, the watershed year back then after which kids could leave school ostensibly fitted for the world. We were studying poetry from one of those textbooks that pander to kids in their format, with cartoons and irregular layout and various fonts and colours, anything to avoid an expanse of print on paper, the greatest cultural invention of all time.

I forget what poems we, or at least I, were looking at but a girl who had already shown herself willing both to have an opinion and to express it asked why pop songs weren't poems. I said that pop songs were indeed poems, but they tended to be crappy ones.

She disagreed. I invited her to give me some lyrics from a pop song so we could study them, and she immediately began to recite and I invited her to come up and write them on the board and I sat at her desk as she did so. The class thought this was all good fun, and as the lyrics appeared on the board one after another in her surprisingly neat hand, they so dripped with cliché –

'Come on, baby, don't be cold as ice' – that I could not resist groaning and encouraging the rest of the class to groan, and then finally she was done and turned to the class and I said, 'So who wrote this stuff?', and she said, 'I did.' And burst into tears.

I've obviously not forgotten it. I hope she has.

Being too easily cowed, and too little endowed with missionary zeal, I was ill suited to teaching at such a school as this. And it depressed me. Ten minutes after the final bell of the day the place was deserted, the staff in their cars having raced the kids on foot to the gates. I lacked the strength of character to defy such an atmosphere, to change things around.

I'd reached a low point. The last eight months had blown my little fantasy out of the water. I had had the time, the space, the money and the freedom to write a good fat novel. I had written a couple of unpublishable poems. I had written less that I'd written when working full time. My thirties were around the corner. It is hard to remember now how ancient thirty seemed. I was already older than Eliot had been when he wrote 'Prufrock': 'I grow old … I grow old … I shall wear the bottoms of my trousers rolled.' And my hair was growing thin. The great redness I had hated as a small boy, that I had pulled out in clumps as a party trick, that I had hacked at with a patented comb-razor, that I had gradually become reconciled to, had started to retreat at the temples, was giving glimpses in the mirror of a pate.

It was a bad time to be looking for teaching jobs, halfway through the academic year. I could find nothing much overseas before September, and in England, well, they wanted an English teacher at short notice at an independent school in Gloucestershire.

I knew at the interview it wasn't for me. The main building was a red-brick Victorian pile. Inside I was assailed by the boarding school smell of floor polish and boiled cabbage. But it was the hushed reverence of the headmaster's secretary, the posh accents and the overwhelming sense of repressed feeling that clamped its claws into my skull. In Canada there had been none of that. And then there was God.

I should perhaps have guessed. The school was named after some otherwise forgotten Victorian clergyman, and the headmaster was desperately keen. He beamed with religious keenness. When he took me on a tour of the school we went at a God-driven trot. He boomed greetings to kids who replied with a polite absence of enthusiasm.

'And can I put you down for any ... mmm ... denomination?' he said when we were back in his study, his pen hovering over a notepad, his head down, hopeful. It took me a few moments to grasp his meaning.

'No,' I said.

He was clearly used to such a response in a heathen age.

'I see from your CV that you have been something of a grasshopper these last few years. How do I know you wouldn't just up sticks again?'

I said something about being back home for good, my wanderlust assuaged, and I'd be willing to sign up for five years there and then.

'No need for signatures,' he said, 'your word is your bond.' He offered me the job, and God help me I took it.

Chapter 30

I was given an attic room in the main building, former maids' quarters. The room alongside mine housed a bluff old bachelor who'd spent his life at the school. He'd been a pupil there and had taught there and had risen to deputy headmaster. He'd left the place only to go to university and war. After retirement he stayed on, presumably because he had nowhere else to go. He ran errands, drove sick children to hospital, oversaw the Alumni Association and was generally a benign presence about the place. His room, as small and eaves-cramped as mine, was lined floor to ceiling with framed photographs of school sports teams.

We shared a small bathroom with no shower. It was the subject of our first conversation, which came almost verbatim from Waugh's *Decline and Fall*.

'I generally take a bath after breakfast,' he said.

'So do I,' I said, though I didn't.

'Oh dear,' he said, as if this was only to be expected in

a world going to the dogs, 'I suppose we'll have to come to some arrangement.'

There was an eerie awfulness about our proximity under the roof. Two men, both single, both houseless, both dependent on the school for food and shelter, separated only by a thin partition wall and forty years. Every morning he woke at six and went in for a bout of coughing that lasted half an hour, coughing of such lung-wrenching ferocity that I feared he might die. Irreversibly woken, I would make a cup of instant coffee and get back into bed with it and smoke and listen to my ancient doppelgänger cough. It felt like the gods having a word.

The old boy was a fixture at dinner in the staffroom. This was a hangover from more formal times when resident staff dined in with silver service, waited on by servants. Now it had shrunk to a white cloth laid over the staffroom table and one of the kitchen hands donning a black and white uniform with apron. You had to wear jacket and tie and the table was presided over by an ancient teacher of French, known universally by a single initial. The third regular was the school organist, a man so chronically shy that he would cross a street to avoid having to say hello, but who played the organ with orgasmic fervour, his hair flying, his shoulders flung and heaving. At dinner he rarely spoke.

The drinks cupboard held only sherry, some thimble-sized glasses and an exercise book with a stub of pencil attached to it by string. If you helped yourself to a glass you were supposed to write it down, to be collated at the end of term and charged for.

The food was good, and free to resident staff, which was the attraction, and the people there meant well, but it was a distillation of everything I'd enjoyed being away from overseas.

Once the subject of women's cricket arose. 'Women can't bowl,' said the former deputy head.

'Really?' I said.

'With the exception of one slow left-armer I saw in Australia, women simply can't bowl.'

'Why not?'

'You don't think I'm going to discuss it over dinner, do you?'

When he said Australia the first three letters rhymed with horse. When he said bowl you could hear the 'w'.

Another time, apropos of I no longer remember what, I asked whether Bombay was a port.

'Oh, Bombay's a port all right. My cricket bag was blown up there in '41.'

It was all too much. But the worst of it was God.

I had always understood that the English upper classes saw the church as more social than religious. At school you learned a set of protocols that meant you belonged to the right crowd, but there was no requirement to actually believe. Indeed it would be rather unseemly to do so, rather infra dig. And I suspect that was how it was for many of the long-serving staff. But the headmaster believed with a passion. He was a lay preacher and he yearned to bring children to Jesus.

At my first staff meeting he announced that a fourth-form girl had died during the holidays. He took possession of the death, forbidding the staff to say anything about it to the kids until he had addressed the school himself in chapel. I found that odd at the time, disturbing now.

A few kids caught the bug of religiosity, as is not unusual in adolescence, but most remained cheerfully heathen. A star pupil, Briony, came shyly to me at the beginning of a lesson and asked if she could leave early as she had an appointment to be baptised. Where was this taking place? The swimming pool, she said.

Confident from her work on *King Lear* that she was doing this only to please assorted adults, I asked her the next day how it had gone. She said with a shy smile that it had gone fine. It transpired that the deed was done by a two-man tag team of the headmaster and the chaplain who stood, together with the baptisee, in the shallow end of the pool.

I asked what the headmaster was wearing.

'A suit,' she said.

'I see,' I said, feeling very pleased with the straightness of my face. 'And the chaplain?'

'A cassock. But with little weights around the hem to stop it floating upwards,' said the observant Briony.

It was this same chaplain – an oleaginous young man with an improbably smooth beard – who once came up to me in the staffroom when I was seething about some now forgotten matter, laid a hand on my forearm in a manner that made me shudder and said, in his oiled-for-Jesus voice, 'Joe, this life is only a rehearsal.'

I made only one friend, Harry, a handsome young teacher of Classics, with patrician vowels, an unfeigned delight in the kids and the sort of fearless disregard for authority that I have always admired. A little drunk one night, we climbed some scaffolding onto the roof of what I think was to become a new gymnasium. A torch beam stabbed up from below accompanied by the voice of the deputy head, a man with whom I did not get on. 'Right, you boys, come on down.' Crouched behind a sort of balustrade I was scared but Harry was giggling.

We stayed up there for fifteen minutes, with the torch

beam playing occasionally along the balustrade as in a bad war movie, then climbed back down the other side. In chapel the next morning, which doubled as school assembly, the head announced that two boys had been observed last night on the roof of the new gymnasium. 'We know who you are. You have until morning break to come forward. After that you will be fetched.'

Harry didn't seem to find the school repressive, perhaps because he had been educated somewhere similar. He and his fiancée Deborah had two red setters, a cat and a pair of lovebirds. One evening we all went out to dinner, came back to their cottage and the cat had somehow opened the cage and killed the lovebirds. Both Harry and Deborah wept. When they finally got married they set up their first house by going around every department store in Gloucester, taking out a store credit card, maxing it out, then cutting it up. By the time they reached the last store there was nothing more they wanted. They bought an electric can opener, and spent the balance on pink champagne.

I taught in a temporary classroom on the edge of a playing field known – and this seems somehow indicative of the whole private school system – as Humpty Dumpty. I liked the isolation from the main buildings, the sense of establishing my own little kingdom, and I got on well enough with the head of English who taught next door. Until, that is, I walked in on him combing his hair in front of a mirror in the book cupboard and made a little joke of it. Ah well.

By and large I enjoyed the teaching. I had only one term to get my upper-sixth class through A level, and they were worryingly unfamiliar with the set texts, but we laughed a lot and most in the end passed, including one lad with a double-barrelled name whose first essay has stayed with me. This was his twelfth and final year of expensive private education and the handwritten essay, which was three sides in length, contained a total of, including the terminal one, two full stops. And no paragraphs. On questioning he admitted that several teachers had mentioned this sort of thing before, 'but, well, you know how it is, sir.' (His name is sufficiently distinctive for me to have just found him with ease on the internet. Aged fifty-something now, he is the CEO of a substantial company.)

That summer Mike Friend was overseeing a language school like the ones we'd worked at together. I went over for a day to teach his teachers, a gang of fresh-faced university students, one of whom had just returned from a gap year in New Zealand, as a resident tutor at Christ's College. 'They're crying out for English teachers over there,' he said, and as he spoke I felt a lurch in my chest. I had little interest in New Zealand, but it wasn't Gloucestershire. And it was very nearly Australia.

Back in Gloucestershire soon afterwards I had a disagreement with the deputy head about some point of organisation of junior sport, and he replied, in the manner of one addressing a bumptious nine-year-old, 'Joe, I've been doing it this way for twenty-five years.' That clinched it, as far as he was concerned. As far as I was concerned, too.

In my attic room that evening I took time over my letter of application. I wrote it in brown ink on pink notepaper. 'Dear Sir,' it began, 'This is an unsolicited request for a job and you'd be well advised to throw it in the bin.' I reasoned that I'd be happy to work for any headmaster who took that bait. No longer remembering the exact name of the school, nor the city in which it stood, I addressed the envelope to 'The Headmaster, Christ's School, New Zealand', sealed it, kissed it and walked it to a pillar box some distance from the school. That same week I applied for a job in Peru. I wanted exile.

Perhaps a month later the phone rang. 'Mr Bennett?' The voice was deep and antipodean. 'Max Rosser, Christ's College. Keep your head down, Mr Bennett, the red tape is flying.'

The sense of a weight being lifted was immediate. I went to the head the next day to resign. He took it well.

Chapter 31

I was also offered the job in Peru. I yearned to take it. It felt exotic. I wanted to take siestas again, to speak Spanish. But it was a bad time. The Shining Path guerrillas controlled much of the country and the local currency in which the salary was offered was suffering from such hyper-inflation as to be worthless. Out of timidity I said no, and Peru became a road not taken, though thought about often enough since.

A teacher from Christ's College came to the UK on holiday. Tasked with running an eye over me, he suggested we meet at a gentlemen's club in Mayfair. The place was like something out of Wodehouse. Fat old men in wingback armchairs snored behind copies of *The Times*. The servants wore white jackets and carried salvers.

'Sorry I'm late,' said my future colleague, who was very late indeed, 'we've been to chiss.'

'We' meant him and his mother. Chiss, I realised only a few hours later when I was on my way back to Gloucestershire, meant the well-known musical.

They were due to fly from Heathrow within a few hours. I had a car now, an elderly Ford Escort, a gift from Keith, who'd graduated to a company car. I had spent long solitary evenings driving it slowly around the school campus, reversing into tight places, doing hill starts and three-point turns, to such good effect that I passed the test at the third attempt. I offered to drive them to the airport, where we could talk at leisure after they'd checked in. Their combined luggage turned out to be a few pounds overweight.

'Mother will sort that out,' my future colleague said, and he left her on her knees in the concourse, going through their suitcases, while we went to the bar to conduct an interview of sorts. He did the talking. I paid for the drinks.

I flew to Auckland in January 1987. I had to borrow the airfare. Thus, after seven years of working life, I arrived in New Zealand on a Sunday morning just as I'd arrived in Spain and France and Canada, with a single suitcase and in debt. I knew nothing of the country. One man who claimed to have been there told me milk was free. And New Zealand House told me there were thirty sheep for every man, woman and child.

When the plane came to a halt I stood up and was told to sit back down. Two grown men in very short shorts came down the aisle spraying aerosols left and right as if in some improbable hijack. An hour later I was walking between the terminals in the startling morning light. The sun seemed to pierce deep into my skin. I thought the cabbage trees were palms.

At the domestic terminal I ordered a coffee. The girl in the kiosk put a level teaspoon of instant powder into a smoked-glass cup, filled it from a boiler on the wall that could have powered the *Titanic* and gestured to a jug of milk on the counter with a little weighted doily over it.

In Christchurch the headmaster met me at the airport and we drove down Memorial Avenue with magisterial slowness. Sprinklers made rainbows on the lawns. There was nobody about. If I was looking for the land without Sundays I hadn't found it.

I was given lunch in a housemaster's garden that ran prettily down to the Avon. I went down by the river to smoke. Under the bank were half a dozen good-sized trout. 'Tiddlers,' said the housemaster. 'Come fishing with us later in the year. I'll show you trout.' And he did. One of my enduring images of the country is of John on the Tekapo River, pointing out fish in the glittering ripple, fish that I'd be unable to make out, and he would pay out line and dry-cast four five six times with his battered split-cane rod before unfurling a black gnat – always a black gnat – onto the water's surface as gently as a kiss and suddenly his reel was screaming and the rod bent like a railway arch. This was fishing as I had never known it, never dreamed of knowing it.

That first afternoon I walked into town to buy provisions. Cathedral Square was hot, empty and shut. I asked a woman in a thick coat for directions to a supermarket and she sent me, after long thought, to Johnson's grocers, which proved to be like something out of the nineteenth century, its window stuffed with British brands I didn't know were still made. And it was shut.

I was a boarding house tutor once again, an assistant, living among the kids. I struggled with their vowels. Ben Wilson, for example, would be Bin Wulson. But he would also, in all probability, be an easy-going farmer's son, who laughed readily, ran barefoot on sports day, loved his rugby and could wire a fence and shear a sheep.

But it was still Australia that I needed to see, that had dragged me aound the world. When I bought a car it was a huge old Holden, because Carl, who'd been there, told me it was just the vehicle to drive the outback in, one elbow crooked out the window. And as Easter approached

I went to Thomas Cook's in Armagh Street to book the car on the ferry to Sydney. The twenty-year-old travel agent put me right with a generously straight face.

On the first day of the holiday I touched down on Australian soil. I went to see Bondi Beach and Darling Harbour and the Sydney Cricket Ground from which John Arlott had broadcast, and it was all, by and large, as envisaged. On a train out to Broken Hill I fell asleep with my head against the juddering glass, and when I awoke it was to the sight of a mob of kangaroos. Shortly afterwards, a pair of emus. It felt as if Australia was offering its totems to be ticked off.

Broken Hill was hot. There was Aboriginal art in the galleries and there were Aboriginal people on the streets. I rented a battered Datsun and drove a dusty side road into the outback for half a tank's worth. Then I stopped the car and got out. Red desert. Dried watercourses. Odd bits of parched scrub. And nothing but more of the same to the horizon in all directions. The land seemed to thrum.

I hitched to Adelaide. My first driver dropped me at a junction about an hour out of Broken Hill. As he pulled away he said he'd be coming back past in a day or two. If I was still there he'd pick me up. We both laughed. A couple of hours later I was feeling nervous. I had a bottle of water and some chocolate and nowhere to go if it got dark. But a woman in a ute stopped and drove me all the way to Adelaide. 'Couldn't leave you there for the snakes,' she said. She pronounced snakes snikes.

In Melbourne I attended an Aussie Rules game at the MCG, a semi-final. The place was full, a hundred thousand people, and I the only one without beer. After the game I waded out through calf-deep cans.

Later in New Zealand a map revealed that I had bitten off only a tiny fraction of the great Australian continent, that the thrumming red heart I'd got a sniff of around Broken Hill extended for unimaginable distances. But I'd seen all I needed to. I'd laid a ghost. The one country I had yearned to visit as a kid, that I had hopelessly set out for after leaving school, that had defined my notion of elsewhere, was just as I'd imagined it. I felt no need to go back.

I turned thirty that month. That first digit is a knell. Where was there to go after thirty? Where was there to go after New Zealand? To step off these islands in any direction was to start to go home. I had been teaching for most of my adult life, but what had I learned? What did I know at thirty that I didn't at, say, ten? Only perhaps that feelings are the ringmaster. They run the show. The rest is fiddlededee.

At the end of the year I borrowed money and bought a semi-derelict cottage in Lyttelton. On the day I moved in I shoved an elbow through the plasterboard because I could, because for the first time in my life a wall was mine.

A year or two further on I went looking for a dog. I'd always promised myself a dog. I went to see several and liked them all but they weren't right. Then I called at a house in Corsair Bay and the dog that stuck his head over the fence was a cream-coloured mongrel. His name was Abel. I had a house and a dog, and, well, that was that, really. It was all over.

Acknowledgements

I'd like to thank Anna Rogers for her wise editing and Alex Hedley for his great patience.